DESTINY LOVERS

Story by Kazutaka

Art by Kai Tomohiro

02

DESTINY LOVERS

CONTENTS

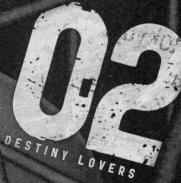

0.2

DESTINY LOVERS

SHIT! ALL OF A SUDDEN...
IT'S GETTING FREEZ-ING IN HERE!!
I APOLOGIZE, BUT WE'RE XPERIENCING PROBLEMS ITH THE AIR CONDITION-ING.
UNTIL IT CAN BE FIXED...
SHE SAID WE'D FREEZE ALIVE IN THIS ICE BOX OF A ROOM.
LET US USE OUR BODY HEAT TO KEEP EACH OTHER WARM.
PLEASE, HELP US THROUGH THE COLD?
SHWIFF...

CHAPTER 10: COLD VS. WARM

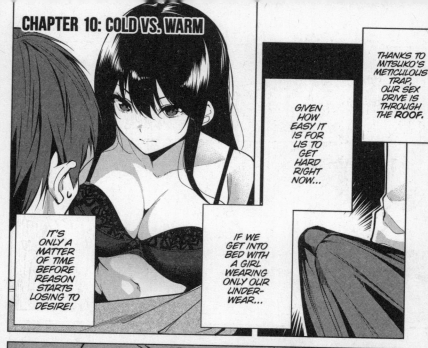

THANKS TO MITSUKO'S METICULOUS TRAP, OUR SEX DRIVE IS THROUGH THE ROOF.

GIVEN HOW EASY IT IS FOR US TO GET HARD RIGHT NOW...

IF WE GET INTO BED WITH A GIRL WEARING ONLY OUR UNDER-WEAR...

IT'S ONLY A MATTER OF TIME BEFORE REASON STARTS LOSING TO DESIRE!

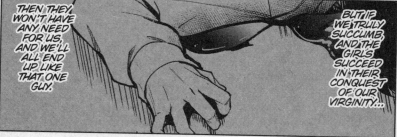

THEN THEY WON'T HAVE ANY NEED FOR US, AND WE'LL ALL END UP LIKE THAT ONE GUY.

BUT IF WE TRULY SUCCUMB, AND THE GIRLS SUCCEED IN THEIR CONQUEST OF OUR VIRGINITY...

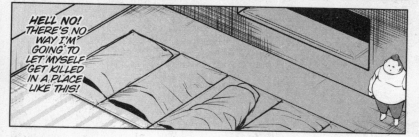

HELL NO! THERE'S NO WAY I'M GOING TO LET MYSELF GET KILLED IN A PLACE LIKE THIS!

EVERYONE! NO MATTER WHAT, DON'T GIVE IN!!
BRR... IT'S FREEZING.
FWSH
PLEASE, WARM ME UP? ♡
I'M GOING TO FREEZE TO DEATH LIKE THIS... ♡
WE DON'T KNOW MUCH ABOUT THIS BOY BESIDES HIS AGE...
BUT GIVEN HOW HARD AND HORNY HE IS...
THERE'S NO WAY A HEALTHY BODY LIKE HIS COULD RESIST!!
SHFF...
SQUISH ♡
SEE?

SQUISH
もみゅ
I'VE GOTTEN COLD HERE, TOO...
AHH... ♡
SQUISH
もみゅっ
AAAH...
GOT HIM NOW!
WHY DON'T YOU WARM ME UP A LITTLE MORE... DIRECTLY?
ぷるんっ
SHWOOP
AHN...!
JOLT
ゾクッ
NNH! ♡
JOLT
ゾクッ
YEAH... ♡ LIKE THAT... ♡
THERE... MORE... ♡
TWEAK...
YESSSS... ♡

TWEAK...
TWEAK
JOLT
HUFF...
AHN...!
......
MMN...♡
HEY.
WHATEVER HAPPENED TO WARMING EACH OTHER UP?
WH- WHAT SHOULD I DO?
......

HM? DID...DID I SAY SOMETHING WRONG?
UH, NO, IT'S NOT LIKE THAT.
IS SHE REALLY THIS INEXPERIENCED, OR SIMPLY DAFT?
ACTUALLY, THIS MAKES THINGS EASIER.
?
HONESTLY, THIS GIRL ISN'T MY TYPE AT ALL.
BUT EVEN IN THIS SITUATION...
I'M STILL AS HARD AS A ROCK!!
DA-DUN

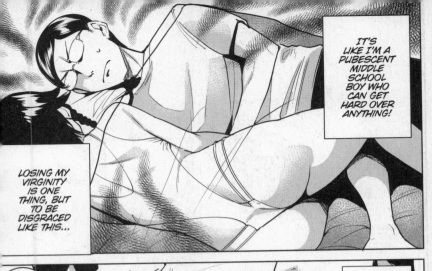

IT'S LIKE I'M A PUBESCENT MIDDLE SCHOOL BOY WHO CAN GET HARD OVER ANYTHING!

LOSING MY VIRGINITY IS ONE THING, BUT TO BE DISGRACED LIKE THIS...

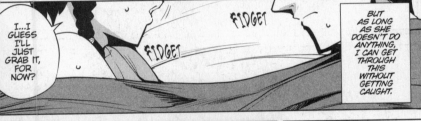

I...I GUESS I'LL JUST GRAB IT, FOR NOW?

FIDGET

FIDGET

BUT AS LONG AS SHE DOESN'T DO ANYTHING, I CAN GET THROUGH THIS WITHOUT GETTING CAUGHT.

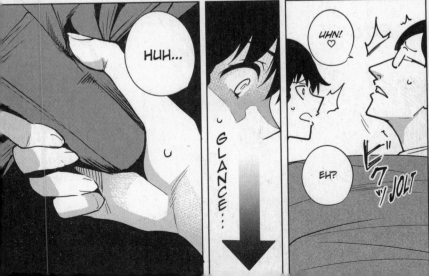

HUH...

GLANCE...

UHN! ♥

EH?

JOLT

I... UH...
BLUUUUUSH...
かあ〜〜〜ッ

STARE...

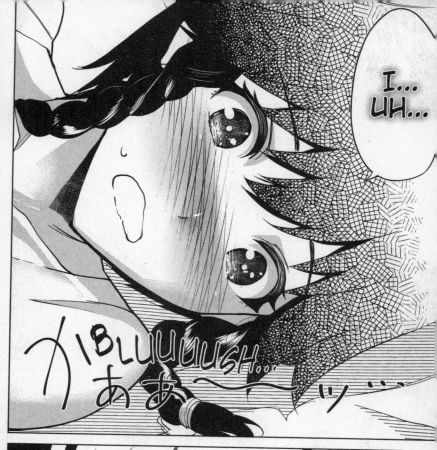

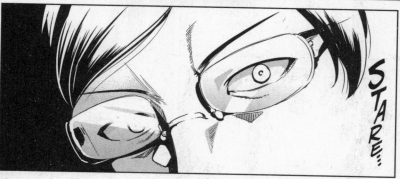

SO, SAYAKA-CHAN...
YOU'RE NOT GOING TO TRY ANY-THING?
HONESTLY, I REALLY HAVE NO CLUE WHAT YOU'RE THINKING.
....
BUT...

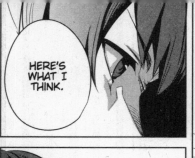

HERE'S WHAT I THINK.

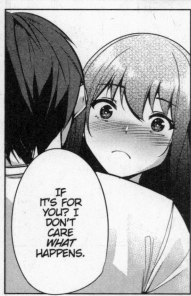

IF IT'S FOR YOU? I DON'T CARE *WHAT* HAPPENS.

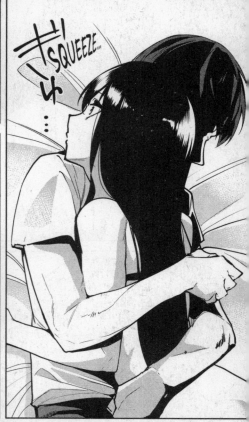

SQUEEZE...

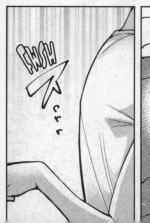

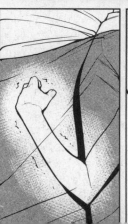

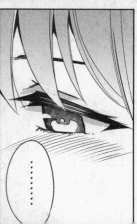

....

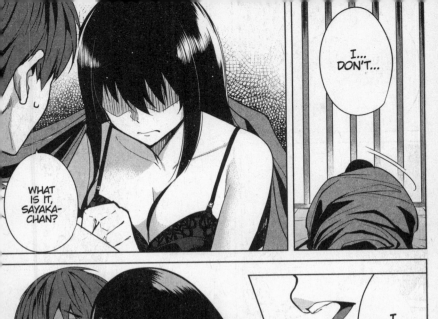

I....
DON'T...

WHAT IS IT, SAYAKA-CHAN?

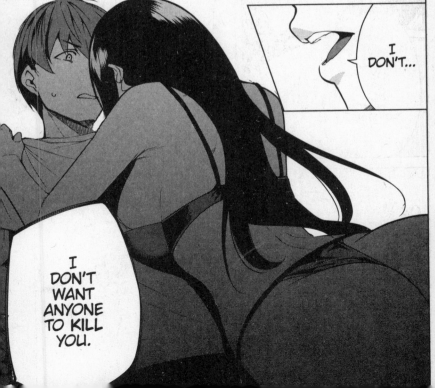

I DON'T...

I DON'T WANT ANYONE TO KILL YOU.

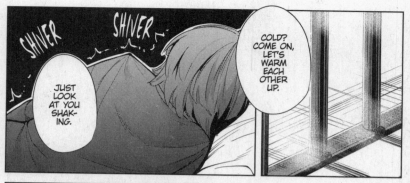

SHIVER SHIVER

COLD? COME ON, LET'S WARM EACH OTHER UP.

JUST LOOK AT YOU SHAK-ING.

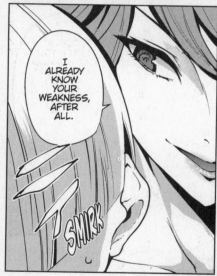

I ALREADY KNOW YOUR WEAKNESS, AFTER ALL.

SMIRK

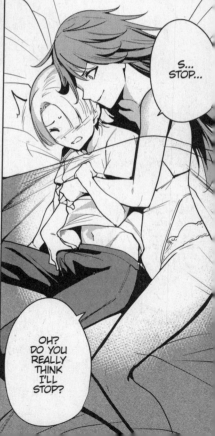

S... STOP...

OH? DO YOU REALLY THINK I'LL STOP?

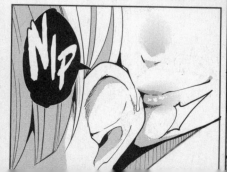

NIP

BLUSH
AH!
YOUR EAR...
LICK
YOU LIKE THIS, DON'T YOU?
......
JOLT
AH... ♡
LOOK AT LITTLE YOU ACTING ALL TOUGH AND HOLDING BACK... COME ON, MORE! ♡
MMN... ♡
RUB
RUB
LET ME HEAR MORE OF YOUR ADORABLE LITTLE WHIMPER-ING!
YOU'RE ALL MINE.
YOU'RE GONNA WANT IT SO BAD.
SHUDDER

IT WOULD BE A SHAME TO END THIS ALL AT ONCE.
I KNOW!
IT'S ALL RIGHT AS LONG AS IT'S NOT SEX, RIGHT?
HUFF...
HUFF...
IN THAT CASE...
I'LL USE MY MOUTH.

I'LL. JUST.
USE. MY. MOUTH.
WHAT...
WHAT DO YOU MEAN?
WELL, LOOK HERE.
SHFF...
LOOKS LIKE YOU'RE GETTING PRETTY HARD!
SHOVE

CHAPTER 11: COLD VS. WARM (2)

WHAT I MEAN IS THAT I'LL USE MY MOUTH TO GIVE YOU SWEET, SWEET RELEASE.
I'LL SWALLOW UP EVERY-THING YOU'VE GOT DOWN THERE.
S-STOP...
HMM... ♡
YOU'VE GOT A CUTE LITTLE BABY FACE, BUT YOU SURE ARE A BIG BOY WHERE IT COUNTS.
I'LL JUST GO AHEAD AND START...AND YOU CAN FEEL IT GET EVEN BIGGER INSIDE MY MOUTH.
JOLT
AHH...
LICK
YOU'RE GOING TO SHOW ME JUST HOW GOOD YOU FEEL.

HOW GREAT IS THIS?
IT'S LIKE I'M THE ONE CONQUERING YOU.
IT SEEMS EVERYONE ELSE IS ENJOYING THEMSELVES.
HOW ABOUT WE START WARMING EACH OTHER UP AS WELL?
SQUOOSH
H-HEY, MITSUKO!
HUSH NOW... ♡
TALKING TOO MUCH IS JUST GOING TO LET OUT THE HEAT.

IT HASN'T BEEN EASY, HAS IT? TURNING IMPOTENT AT SUCH A YOUNG AGE.
BUT ALL THAT SUFFERING ENDS TODAY.
SEE? IT'S TOUCHING MY STOMACH.
SO BIG...SO VIRILE... ♡
GRIND
ぐいん
GRIND
HERE. ♡
SEE? ♡
LOOK HOW BIG IT IS. ♡
GRIP
スリ…

KNOCK... IT... OFF...
DO YOU REALLY WANT ME TO STOP NOW?
YOU BITCH!
EVEN THOUGH IT'S BEEN SO LONG SINCE YOU'VE BEEN HARD?
EVEN THOUGH I'M ONLY SLIGHTLY BRUSHING IT ON TOP OF YOUR CLOTHES...
AND YOU CAN ALREADY FEEL SO MUCH?
NOW...
SWF...
HOW ABOUT YOU GIVE ME SOME OF YOUR HEAT...? ♡

CAN'T FORGET TO WARM UP YOUR FACE, EITHER...
FLUMP...
AHH, THAT'S THE WAY. ♡ I CAN FEEL MYSELF GETTING WARMER AND WARMER... ♡
FWAP ♡
FWAP
GRIP
OOH. JUST WHAT DOES THAT HAND THINK IT'S DOING?
HUFF...
HUFF...
HUFF...
HUFF...

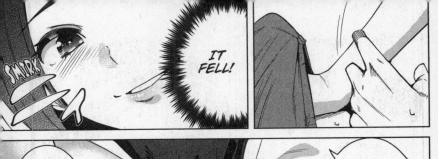

IT FELL!

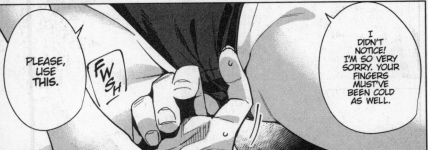

PLEASE, USE THIS.

FWSH

I DIDN'T NOTICE! I'M SO VERY SORRY. YOUR FINGERS MUST'VE BEEN COLD AS WELL.

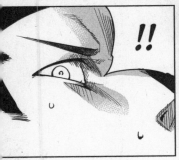

!!

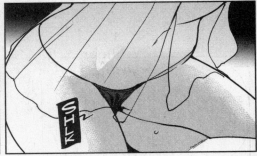

SHLK

YOU... YOU DON'T WANT ANYONE TO KILL ME?

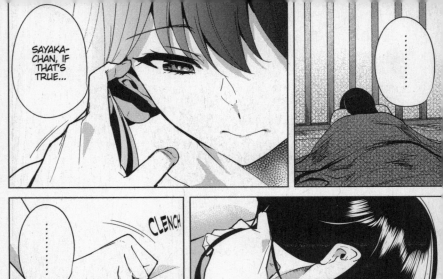

SAYAKA-CHAN, IF THAT'S TRUE...

・・・・・・

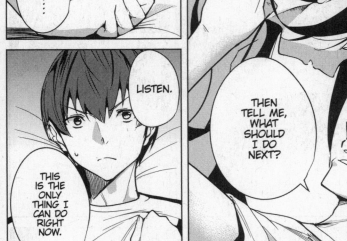

・・・・・・・

CLENCH

LISTEN.

THIS IS THE ONLY THING I CAN DO RIGHT NOW.

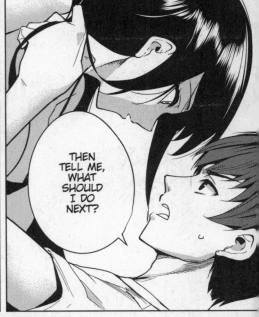

THEN TELL ME, WHAT SHOULD I DO NEXT?

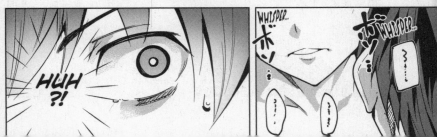

HUH?!

WHISPER...

WHISPER...

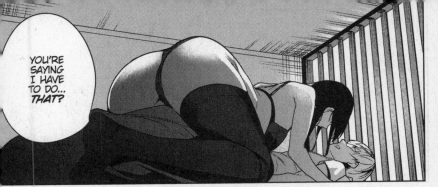

YOU'RE SAYING I HAVE TO DO... *THAT*?

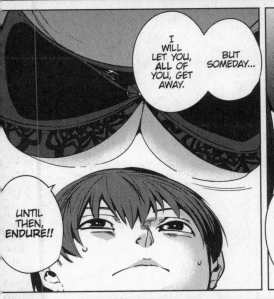

I WILL LET YOU, ALL OF YOU, GET AWAY.

BUT SOMEDAY...

UNTIL THEN, ENDURE!!

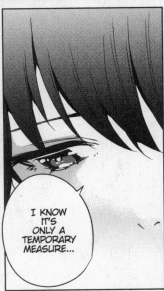

I KNOW IT'S ONLY A TEMPORARY MEASURE...

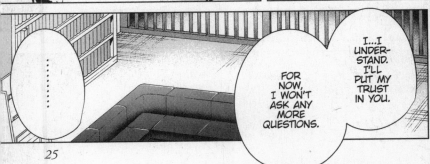

· · · · · · · ·

FOR NOW, I WON'T ASK ANY MORE QUESTIONS.

I...I UNDER-STAND. I'LL PUT MY TRUST IN YOU.

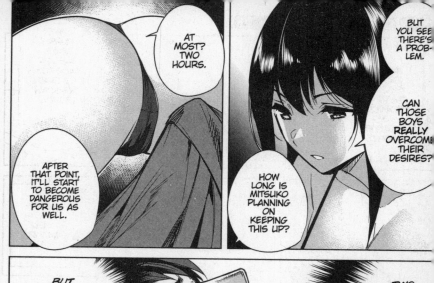

AT MOST? TWO HOURS.

BUT YOU SEE THERE'S A PROBLEM.

CAN THOSE BOYS REALLY OVERCOME THEIR DESIRES?

AFTER THAT POINT, IT'LL START TO BECOME DANGEROUS FOR US AS WELL.

HOW LONG IS MITSUKO PLANNING ON KEEPING THIS UP?

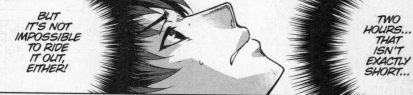

BUT IT'S NOT IMPOSSIBLE TO RIDE IT OUT, EITHER!

TWO HOURS... THAT ISN'T EXACTLY SHORT...

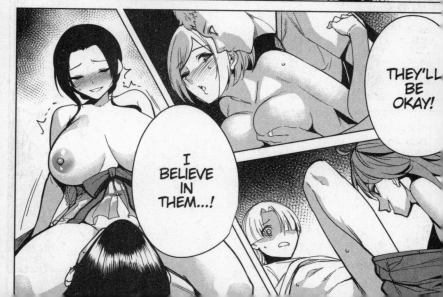

THEY'LL BE OKAY!

I BELIEVE IN THEM...!

CHAPTER 12: COLD VS. WARM (3)

TWO HOURS UNTIL THE AIR CONDITIONER STARTS WORKING AGAIN.
AHN... ♥
MM... ♥
WE JUST HAVE TO FEND OFF THE GIRLS' ADVANCES... NO MATTER WHAT.
HAAH...
EVERYONE-- YOU CAN DO IT!
JOLT
GLANCE...
SERIOUSLY, JUST WHO IS THIS BOY?!
AH! ♥
OOH! ♥
AH! ♥
YES! ♥
THE WAY HE CARESSES MY BOOBS...
SQUIRSH...

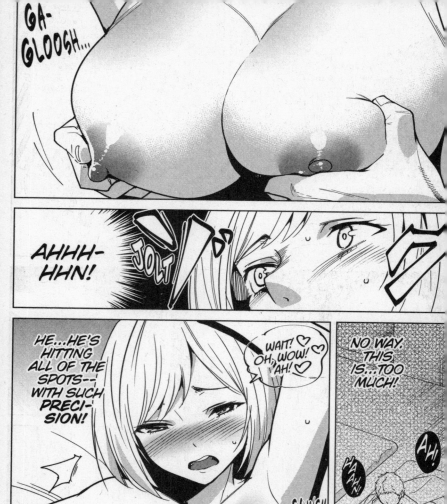

GA-GLOOSH...

AHHH-HHN!

JOLT

HE...HE'S HITTING ALL OF THE SPOTS-- WITH SUCH PRECISION!

WAIT! ♡ OH, WOW! AH! ♡

SAWSH

SAWSH

SAWSH

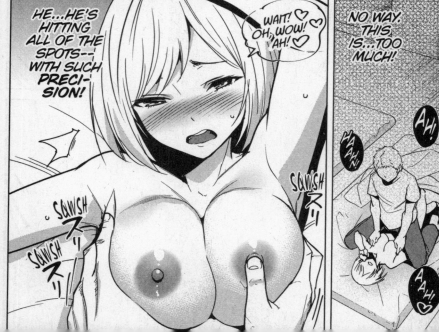

NO WAY. THIS IS...TOO MUCH!

HAAAN!

AH!

AAAH!

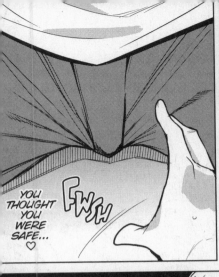

YOU THOUGHT YOU WERE SAFE... ♡

FWSH

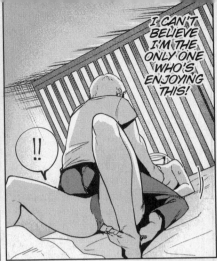

I CAN'T BELIEVE I'M THE ONLY ONE WHO'S ENJOYING THIS!

!!

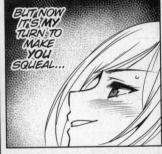

BUT NOW IT'S MY TURN TO MAKE YOU SQUEAL...

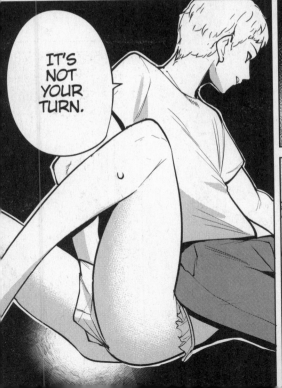

IT'S NOT YOUR TURN.

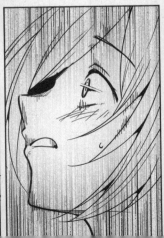

WHAT?! NO WAY!
JOLT
AH!
NH!
NNNGH!
W... WAIT...
SERIOUSLY! PLEASE, JUST NOT SO FAST...!
WHAT... WHAT IS WITH THIS TECH-NIQUE?!
SHLRK...
UNH...
HOO...AHH...!
HE... HE'S GOING TO MAKE ME...
AAAH!
NGH!
AHHN!

SHLUP...
AHHHNN!
JOLT
JOLT
HUFF...
HUFF...
HUFF...

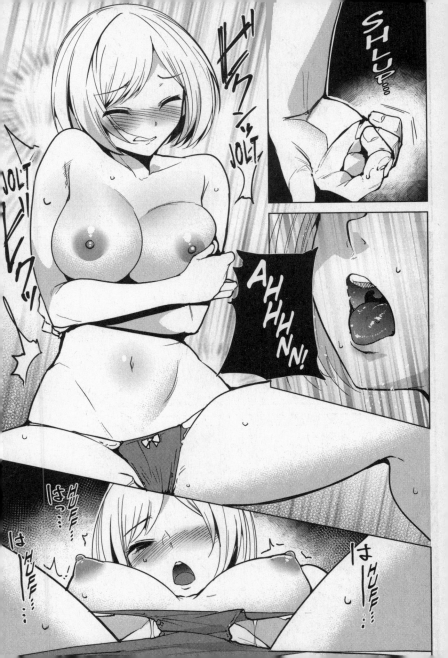

SLFF
P-PLEASE.
DO IT...
I WANT IT... PLEASE. ♡
HUFF...
HUFF...
HUFF...!
FINE.
BUT...
ON ONE CONDI-TION!

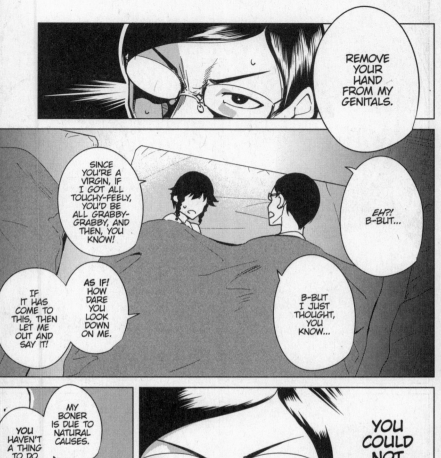

REMOVE YOUR HAND FROM MY GENITALS.

SINCE YOU'RE A VIRGIN, IF I GOT ALL TOUCHY-FEELY, YOU'D BE ALL GRABBY-GRABBY, AND THEN, YOU KNOW!

EH?! B-BUT...

IF IT HAS COME TO THIS, THEN LET ME OUT AND SAY IT!

AS IF! HOW DARE YOU LOOK DOWN ON ME.

B-BUT I JUST THOUGHT, YOU KNOW...

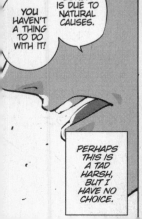

PERHAPS THIS IS A TAD HARSH, BUT I HAVE NO CHOICE.

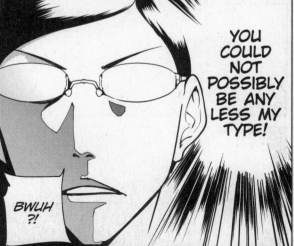

YOU HAVEN'T A THING TO DO WITH IT!

MY BONER IS DUE TO NATURAL CAUSES.

YOU COULD NOT POSSIBLY BE ANY LESS MY TYPE!

BWUH?!

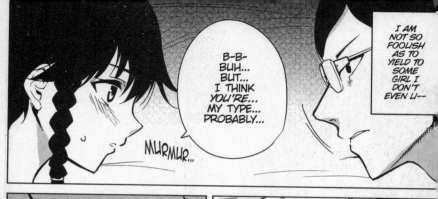

B-B-BUH... BUT... I THINK YOU'RE... MY TYPE... PROBABLY...

I AM NOT SO FOOLISH AS TO YIELD TO SOME GIRL I DON'T EVEN LI--

MURMUR...

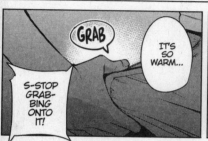

GRAB

IT'S SO WARM...

S-STOP GRABBING ONTO IT!

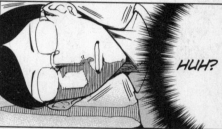

HUH?

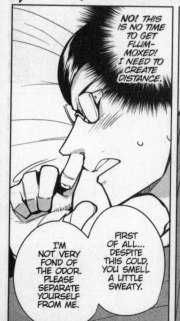

NO! THIS IS NO TIME TO GET FLUMMOXED! I NEED TO CREATE DISTANCE.

I'M NOT VERY FOND OF THE ODOR. PLEASE SEPARATE YOURSELF FROM ME.

FIRST OF ALL... DESPITE THIS COLD, YOU SMELL A LITTLE SWEATY.

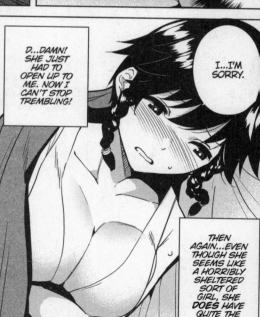

D...DAMN! SHE JUST HAD TO OPEN UP TO ME. NOW I CAN'T STOP TREMBLING!

I...I'M SORRY.

THEN AGAIN...EVEN THOUGH SHE SEEMS LIKE A HORRIBLY SHELTERED SORT OF GIRL, SHE DOES HAVE QUITE THE FIGURE.

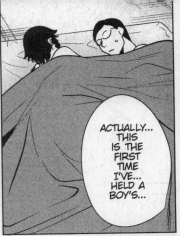

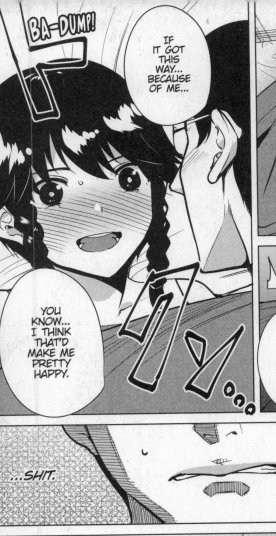

BA-DUMP!

IF IT GOT THIS WAY... BECAUSE OF ME...

ACTUALLY... THIS IS THE FIRST TIME I'VE... HELD A BOY'S...

YOU KNOW... I THINK THAT'D MAKE ME PRETTY HAPPY.

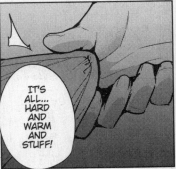

IT'S ALL... HARD AND WARM AND STUFF!

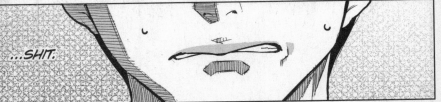

...SHIT.

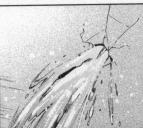

I TRIED TO HOLD BACK MY URGES WITH REASON AND LOGIC, BUT NOW...!

EVEN THE TINIEST HOLE CAN BRING DOWN A WHOLE DAM...

IT'S NOT LIKE I'D BE OKAY WITH JUST ANYONE...
BUT I THOUGHT... IF IT'S SUKEKAWA-SAN, THEN MAYBE...
STOP RIGHT THERE, SELF! NOT ONE STEP FURTHER!
THIS ERECTION IS NOTHING MORE THAN A BIOLOGICAL PROCESS!
BUT GOD DAMN! I STILL WANT TO PUSH HER DOWN AND GET NASTY!
NO! STOP RIGHT THERE! DO NOT GIVE IN TO HER SWEET SIREN'S SONG!
I CAN'T AFFORD IT! THIS MIGHT BE A LIFE OR DEATH SITUATION.
PUSH HER ASIDE! I MUST REFUSE HER ONCE AND FOR ALL!
KER-THUNK
JUST GET AWAY FROM ME ALREADY!
HUH?! WAIT!
I'M SORRY TO BE SO ROUGH, BUT...
SQUOOOSH
HM?

......!
KA-KRAK

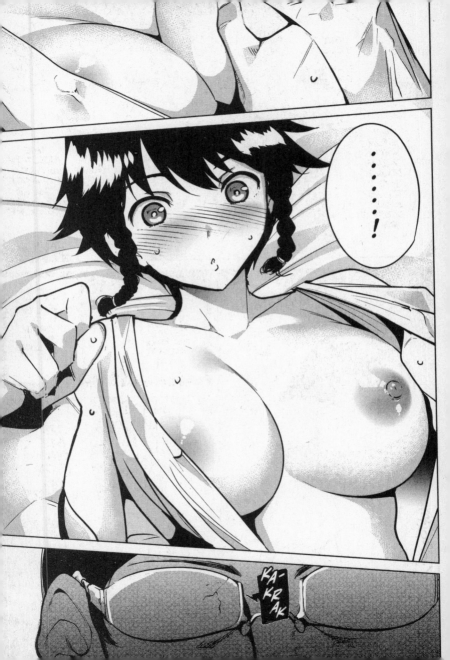

OKAY. ALL RIGHT. THAT'S MY LIMIT.
I GIVE IN.

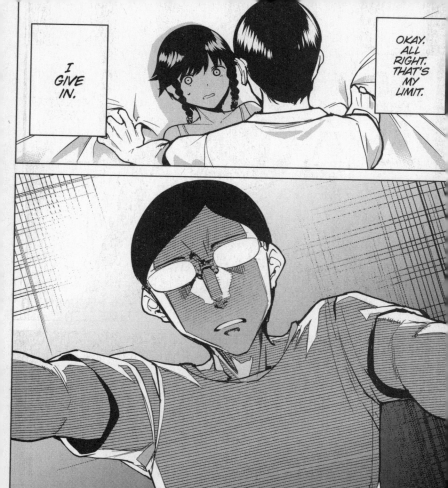

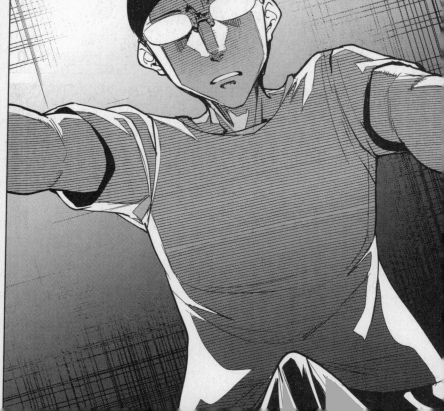

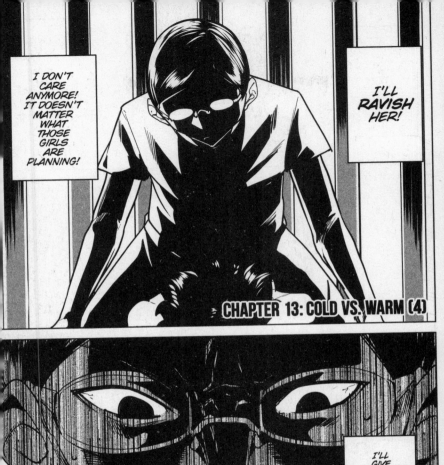

I DON'T CARE ANYMORE! IT DOESN'T MATTER WHAT THOSE GIRLS ARE PLANNING!

I'LL RAVISH HER!

CHAPTER 13: COLD VS. WARM (4)

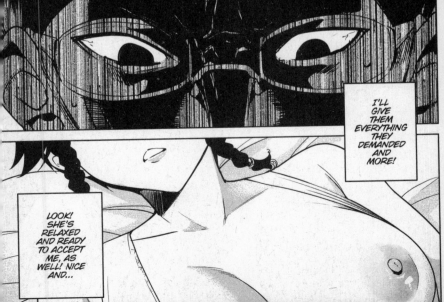

I'LL GIVE THEM EVERYTHING THEY DEMANDED AND MORE!

LOOK! SHE'S RELAXED AND READY TO ACCEPT ME, AS WELL! NICE AND...

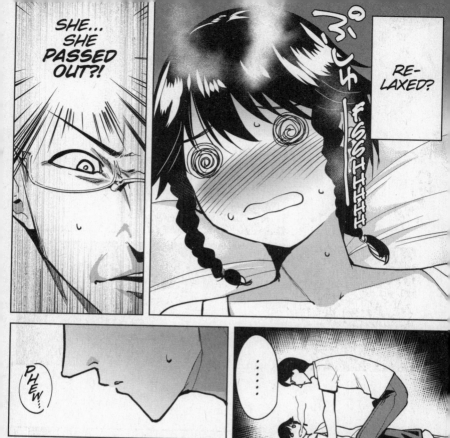

SHE... SHE PASSED OUT?!

RE-LAXED?

PHEW...

. . . . .

THAT WAS CLOSE. I ALMOST COMPLETELY LOST CONTROL!

WHAT ON EARTH WAS I DOING JUST NOW?!

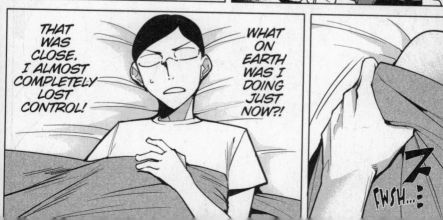

FWSH...

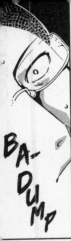

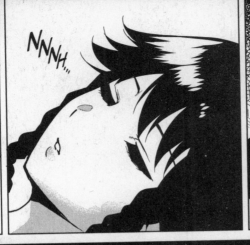

NNNH...

BA-DUMP

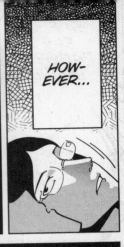

HOW-EVER...

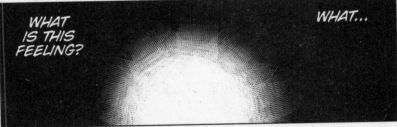

WHAT IS THIS FEELING?

WHAT...

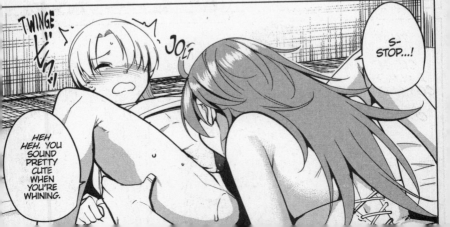

TWINGE

JOLT

S-STOP...!

HEH HEH. YOU SOUND PRETTY CUTE WHEN YOU'RE WHINING.

LICK...
NOW COMES WHAT YOU'VE BEEN WAITING FOR...
SHUDDER
SHLURP
LOOK AT YOU, SO HELPLESS!
JOLT
UHN! ♥
AHH! ♥
JOLT
SHAME, JOY, ECSTASY, HUMILIATION... ALL IN ONE FACE!
COME ON... SHOW ME SOME MORE. REVEL IN IT!

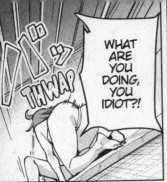

THWAP

WHAT ARE YOU DOING, YOU IDIOT?!

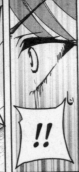

!!

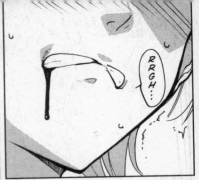

RRGH...

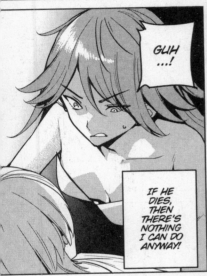

GUH...!

IF HE DIES, THEN THERE'S NOTHING I CAN DO ANYWAY!

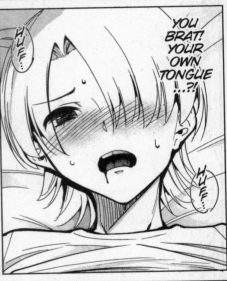

HUFF

HUFF

YOU BRAT! YOUR OWN TONGUE...?!

HUFF

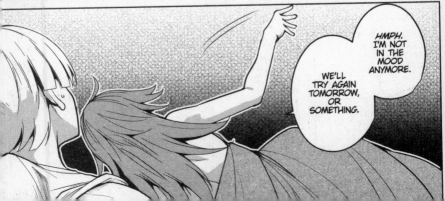

HMPH. I'M NOT IN THE MOOD ANYMORE.

WE'LL TRY AGAIN TOMORROW, OR SOMETHING.

......
WHEW...
WHO WOULD'VE THOUGHT HE'D RESIST ME THIS MUCH?
BUT THIS BOY IS SOME-THING ELSE.
TCH... カリ...
HOW ON EARTH IS HE STILL A VIRGIN, ANYWAY?
JUST LOOK AT HIM. HE'S JUST BEGGING TO BE DOMI-NATED.
TCHI
HOW COULD SOMEONE SO ABSO-LUTELY DELICIOUS STAY A VIRGIN FOR SO LONG?
KAZA-MATSURI SHUNTA...
JUST WHAT ARE YOU HIDING?!

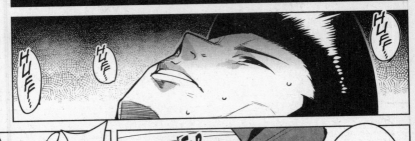

HUFF HUFF HUFF HUFF

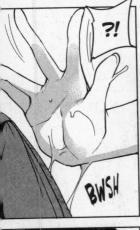

?!

FAP FAP

BWSH

IRABU-SAMA, I DIDN'T KNOW YOU COULD MAKE SUCH A SOUND.

IS IT... ABOUT TIME?

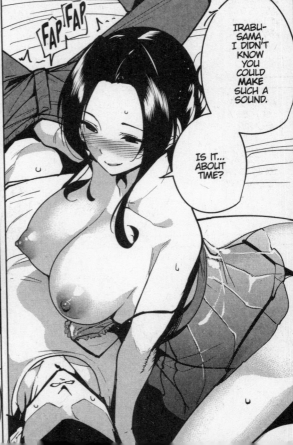

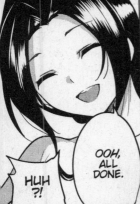

OOH, ALL DONE.

HUH ?!

HUH? DONE?!
NO WAY!!
WHAT'S WITH THAT LONGING FACE?
YOU WANT TO FEEL EVEN BETTER, DON'T YOU?
IN THAT CASE...
FWISH
HOW ABOUT WE JUST SLIDE IT RIGHT IN?

NO... ANYTHING BUT THAT.
READY? ♡
LICK...
HAAH!
SHLRP
SHLRP
HUFF!
HUFF! ♡
SQSH...
GLOP...
SHLP...
DAMN IT! MY BODY, MY MIND... THEY WON'T LISTEN
SHALL WE TAKE THINGS TO THE NEXT LEVEL...?

I'M FINISHED...
DRIP...
SMIRK...
GASP!
IT LOOKS LIKE YOU'RE FINALLY READY. ♡
TOTALLY, COM-PLETELY FUCKED ...!!

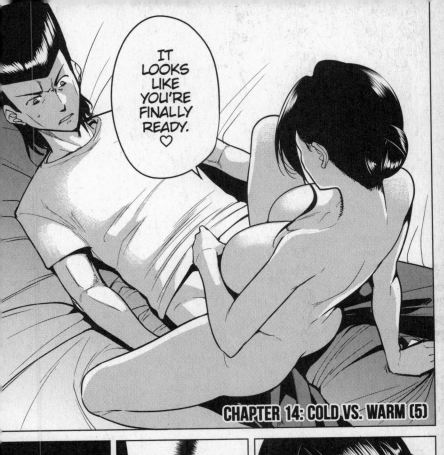

IT LOOKS LIKE YOU'RE FINALLY READY. ♡

CHAPTER 14: COLD VS. WARM (5)

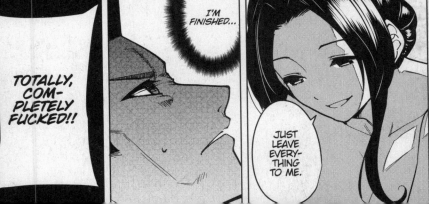

TOTALLY, COMPLETELY FUCKED!!

I'M FINISHED...

JUST LEAVE EVERYTHING TO ME.

I CAN'T BEAR IT ANYMORE...
RUUUUMMMBLE
O... OGA-WARA?!
HURRRPH...
I...
I CAN'T STAND THE COLD ANYMORE!!
WHOOM
JOLT
IRABU! LET'S WARM EACH OTHER UP!
RUB
RUB
RUB
RUB
HEY! THE FUCK YOU DOIN'?!

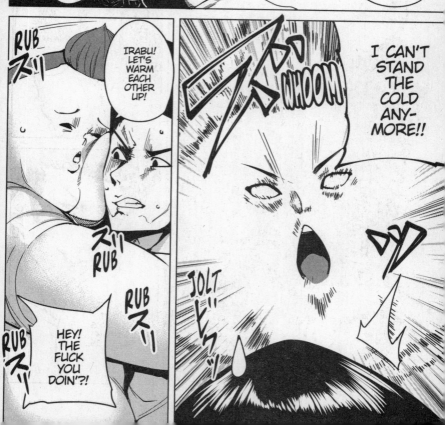

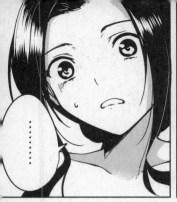

......

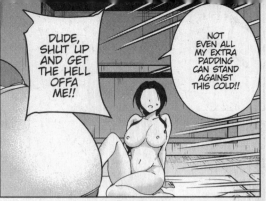

DUDE, SHUT UP AND GET THE HELL OFFA ME!!

NOT EVEN ALL MY EXTRA PADDING CAN STAND AGAINST THIS COLD!!

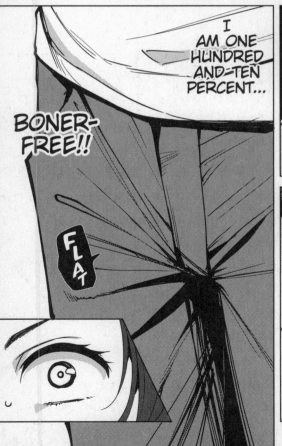

I AM ONE HUNDRED AND-TEN PERCENT...

BONER-FREE!!

FLAT

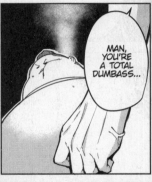

MAN, YOU'RE A TOTAL DUMBASS...

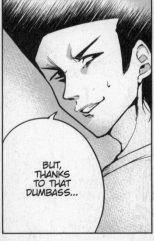

BUT, THANKS TO THAT DUMBASS...

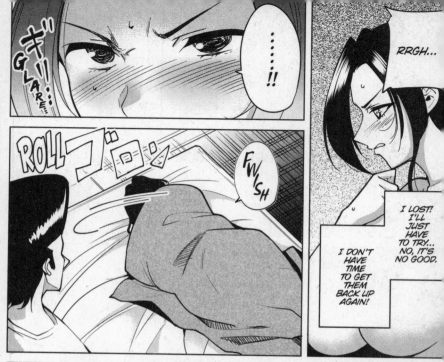

GLARE!!

: : : : : !!

RRGH...

ROLL ゴゴロ゛

FWISH

I LOST! I'LL JUST HAVE TO TRY... NO, IT'S NO GOOD.

I DON'T HAVE TIME TO GET THEM BACK UP AGAIN!

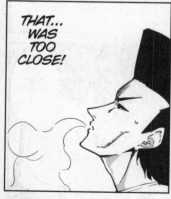

THAT... WAS TOO CLOSE!

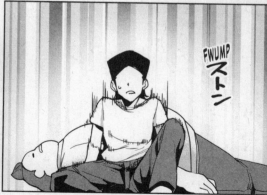

FWUMP ストン

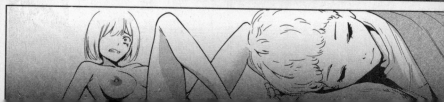

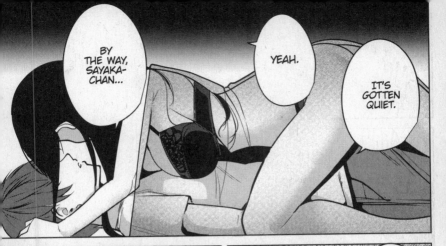

BY THE WAY, SAYAKA-CHAN...

YEAH.

IT'S GOTTEN QUIET.

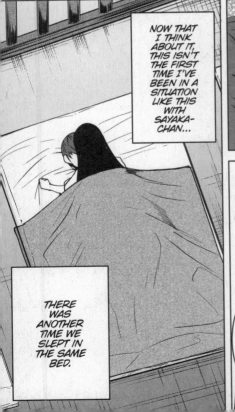

NOW THAT I THINK ABOUT IT, THIS ISN'T THE FIRST TIME I'VE BEEN IN A SITUATION LIKE THIS WITH SAYAKA-CHAN...

THERE WAS ANOTHER TIME WE SLEPT IN THE SAME BED.

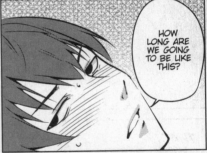

HOW LONG ARE WE GOING TO BE LIKE THIS?

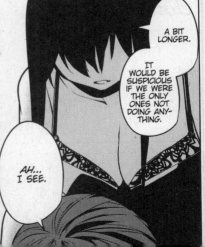

A BIT LONGER.

IT WOULD BE SUSPICIOUS IF WE WERE THE ONLY ONES NOT DOING ANYTHING.

AH... I SEE.

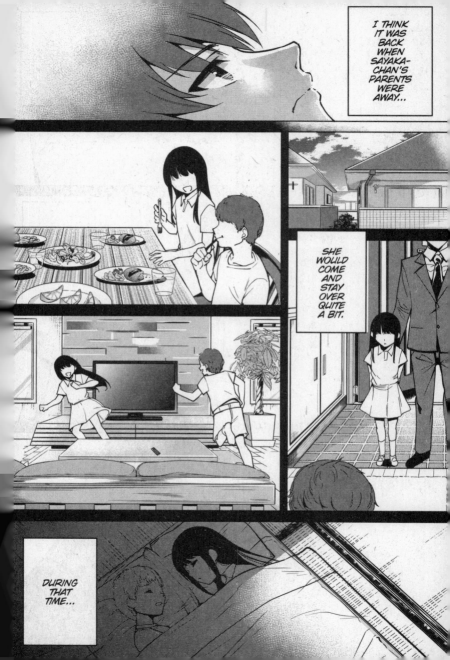

I THINK IT WAS BACK WHEN SAYAKA-CHAN'S PARENTS WERE AWAY...

SHE WOULD COME AND STAY OVER QUITE A BIT.

DURING THAT TIME...

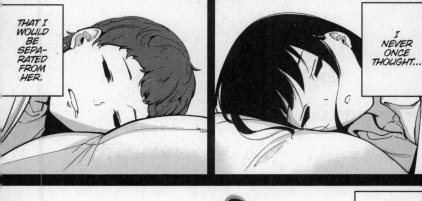

THAT I
WOULD
BE
SEPA-
RATED
FROM
HER.

I
NEVER
ONCE
THOUGHT...

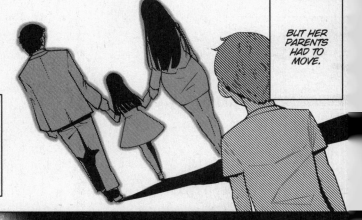

BUT HER
PARENTS
HAD TO
MOVE.

EVEN
APART,
I ALWAYS
BELIEVED
WE'D BE
TOGETHER.

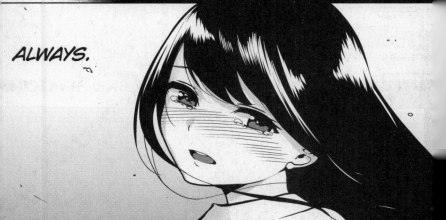

ALWAYS.

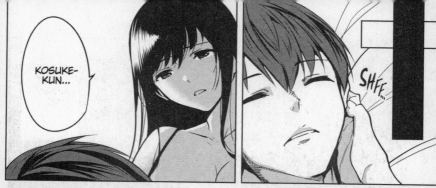

KOSUKE-
KUN...

SHFF...

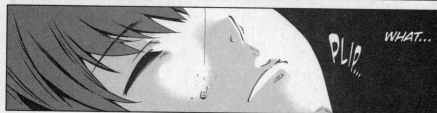

PLIP...

WHAT...

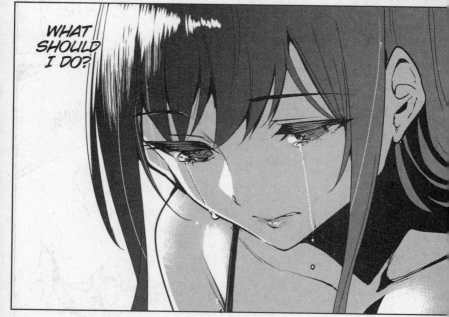

WHAT
SHOULD
I DO?

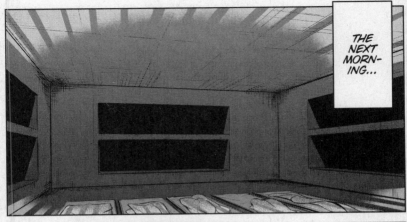

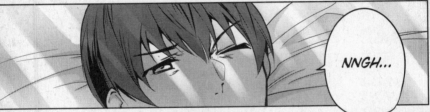

NNGH...

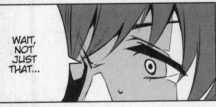

WAIT, NOT JUST THAT...

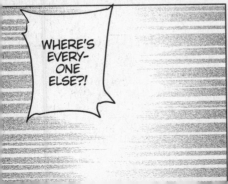

WHERE'S EVERYONE ELSE?!

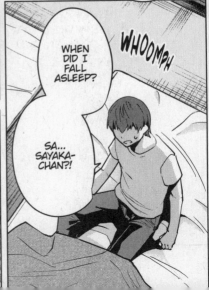

WHEN DID I FALL ASLEEP?

WHOOMPH

SA... SAYAKA-CHAN?!

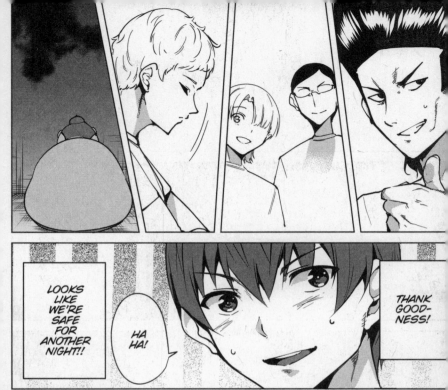

LOOKS LIKE WE'RE SAFE FOR ANOTHER NIGHT!!

HA HA!

THANK GOOD-NESS!

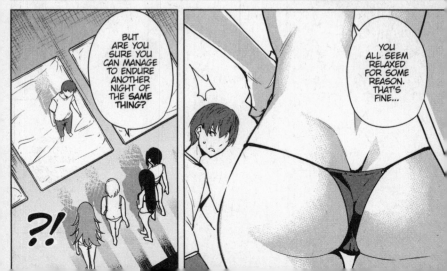

BUT ARE YOU SURE YOU CAN MANAGE TO ENDURE ANOTHER NIGHT OF THE SAME THING?

?!

YOU ALL SEEM RELAXED FOR SOME REASON. THAT'S FINE...

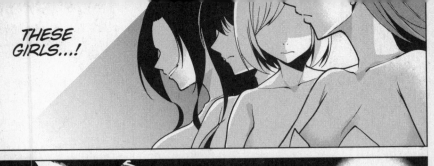

THESE GIRLS...!

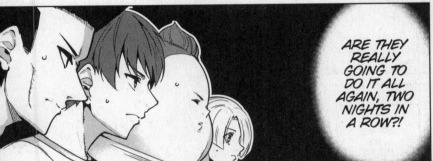

ARE THEY REALLY GOING TO DO IT ALL AGAIN, TWO NIGHTS IN A ROW?!

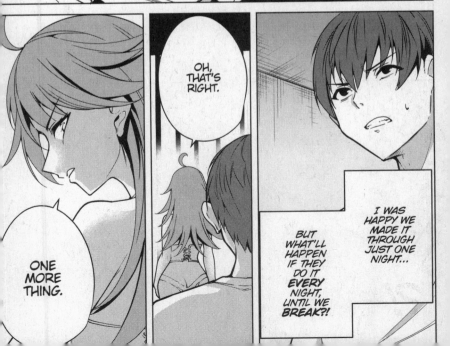

OH, THAT'S RIGHT.

ONE MORE THING.

BUT WHAT'LL HAPPEN IF THEY DO IT EVERY NIGHT, UNTIL WE BREAK?!

I WAS HAPPY WE MADE IT THROUGH JUST ONE NIGHT...

WE'RE WATCHING ALL OF YOU VERY CLOSELY.
DON'T EVEN THINK ABOUT DOING ANYTHING STUPID.
YOU ALL JUST WASH YOUR DICKS AND SIT TIGHT.
GLOOOOOM...
NOW THEN, WE'LL BE SEEING YOU AGAIN LATER...
MY DEAR MASTERS. ♡
NOW WHAT?!
SIXTEEN HOURS REMAIN UNTIL LIGHTS OUT.

CHAPTER 15: GIRLS VS. GIRLS

Locker Room
WE'RE GOING TO TRY AGAIN?
YES.
DON'T WORRY. TONIGHT IS THE NIGHT.
I'M SURE THAT WITH JUST ONE MORE PUSH, WE'LL HAVE THEM.
I'M HAVING DÉJÀ VU OVER HERE. COME ON, YOU FAILED. SAME AS US.
ONLY THANKS TO AN UNEXPECTED INTRUDER.

......
WAS HE... FOR REAL?
I have one condition.
HAAH!♡
And what might that be?
HUFF...♡
Go on. ♡ Come on! ♡ Tell me! ♡
MMN!♡
You have to die.
What ...?

That's my fetish.
I can only do it if the chick's already dead.
DOOOM...
MAYBE HE WAS JUST TRYING TO SHOCK ME...?
HEY, AINA! WHAT ARE YOU DOING OVER THERE?!
I-I'M SORRY, JUST SPACED OUT FOR A BIT.
FAILING GOT YOU DOWN, TOO? THAT'S A LITTLE OUT OF CHARACTER FOR YOU.

I'M FINE!
THIS IS FOR ALL HUMANITY, AFTER ALL.
KER-CHAK
SUCH A PAIN IN THE ASS, THOUGH. I DON'T UNDERSTAND WHY WE CAN'T JUST FORCE 'EM.
LET'S JUST DRUG 'EM UP AND GET THIS OVER WITH!
DID YOU NOT HEAR ME WHEN I SAID THE ORGANIZATION SAID THE USE OF DRUGS IS PROHIBITED?
I KNOW, I JUST DON'T GET *WHY* WE HAVE TO WAIT FOR THEM TO GET IN THE MOOD.

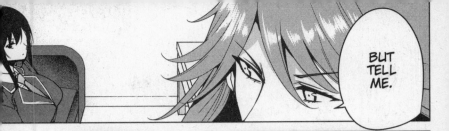

BUT TELL ME.

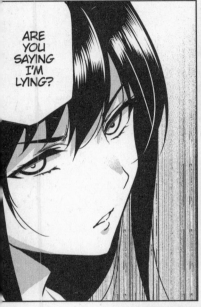

ARE YOU SAYING I'M LYING?

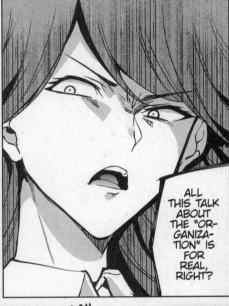

ALL THIS TALK ABOUT THE "OR-GANIZA-TION" IS FOR REAL, RIGHT?

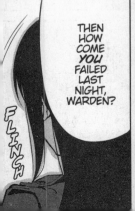

THEN HOW COME *YOU* FAILED LAST NIGHT, WARDEN?

FLINCH

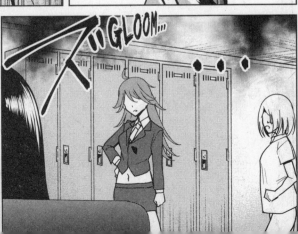

GLOOM...

DIDN'T THAT BOY ASK FOR YOU BY NAME?
SHOULDN'T HE HAVE BEEN EASY PICKINGS?
I HAVE NO REASON NOR DESIRE TO NEEDLESSLY DEFEND MYSELF TO YOU.
....
CLAP
CLAP
THAT'S ENOUGH.

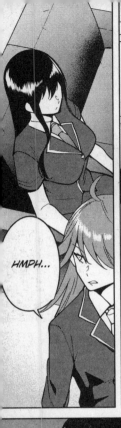

HMPH...

THERE'S NO POINT IN US FIGHTING.

IT'LL BE SETTLED TONIGHT ANYWAY.

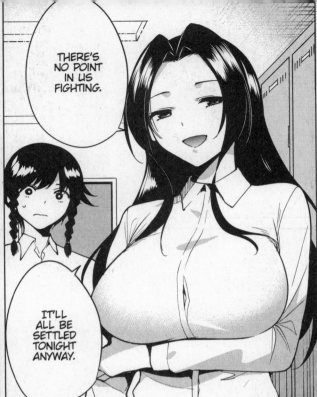

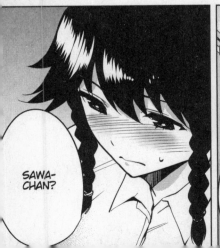

SAWA-CHAN?

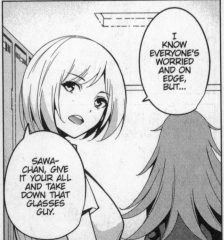

I KNOW EVERYONE'S WORRIED AND ON EDGE, BUT...

SAWA-CHAN, GIVE IT YOUR ALL AND TAKE DOWN THAT GLASSES GUY.

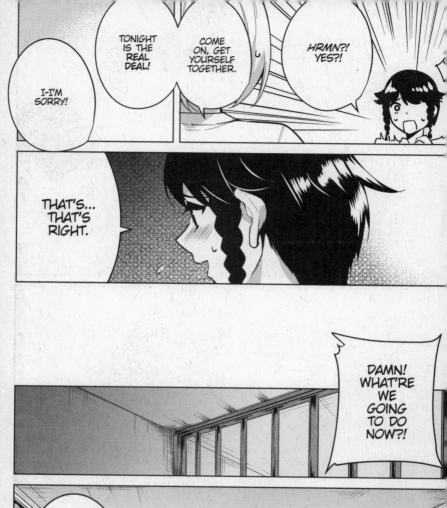

HRMN?! YES?!
COME ON, GET YOURSELF TOGETHER.
TONIGHT IS THE REAL DEAL!
I-I'M SORRY!
THAT'S... THAT'S RIGHT.
DAMN! WHAT'RE WE GOING TO DO NOW?!
TO THINK THEY WOULD ALREADY COME AGAIN TONIGHT...

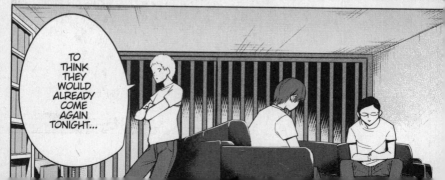

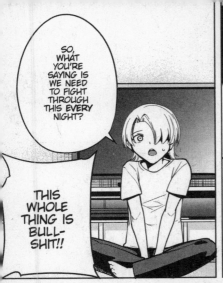

SO, WHAT YOU'RE SAYING IS WE NEED TO FIGHT THROUGH THIS EVERY NIGHT?

THIS WHOLE THING IS BULL-SHIT!!

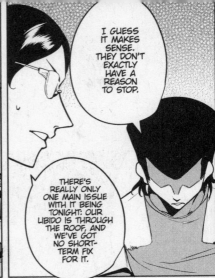

I GUESS IT MAKES SENSE. THEY DON'T EXACTLY HAVE A REASON TO STOP.

THERE'S REALLY ONLY ONE MAIN ISSUE WITH IT BEING TONIGHT: OUR LIBIDO IS THROUGH THE ROOF, AND WE'VE GOT NO SHORT-TERM FIX FOR IT.

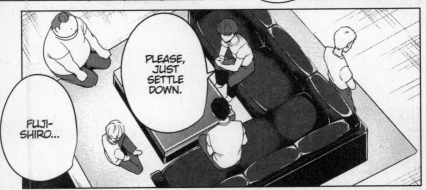

PLEASE, JUST SETTLE DOWN.

FUJI-SHIRO...

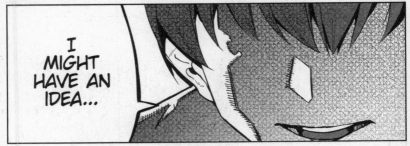

I MIGHT HAVE AN IDEA...

?!
WE'RE ALL GOING TO MASTUR-BATE!!

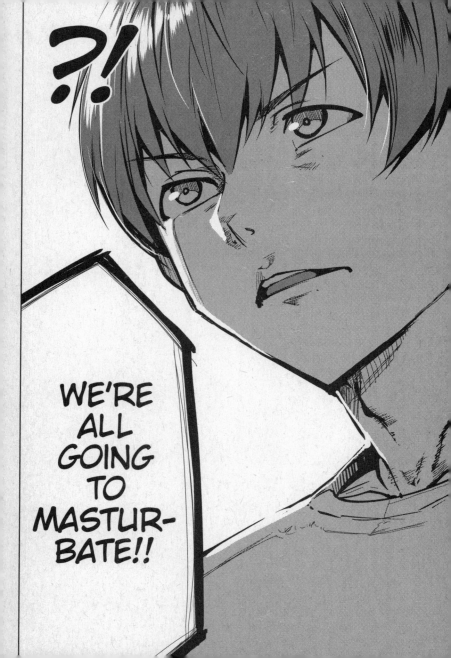

02

DESTINY LOVERS

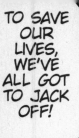

TO SAVE OUR LIVES, WE'VE ALL GOT TO JACK OFF!

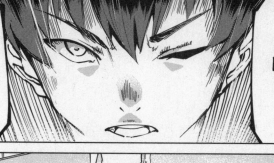

YOU HEARD ME!

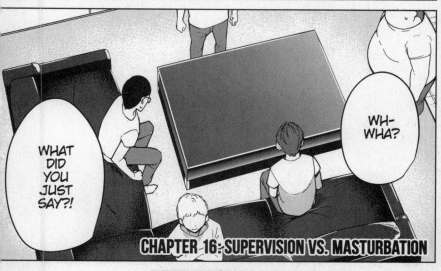

WHAT DID YOU JUST SAY?!

WH-WHA?

CHAPTER 16: SUPERVISION VS. MASTURBATION

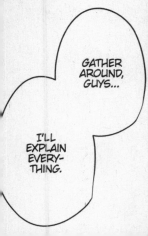

GATHER AROUND, GUYS...

I'LL EXPLAIN EVERY-THING.

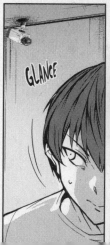

GLANCE

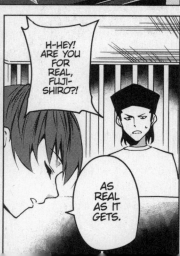

H-HEY! ARE YOU FOR REAL, FUJI-SHIRO?!

AS REAL AS IT GETS.

FIRST, LET'S GO OVER WHAT WE KNOW.
THE GIRLS' GOAL IS TO CLAIM THE VIRGINITY OF US, THE CAPTIVE VIRGINS.
THE REASON IS UNCLEAR, BUT THEY DID SAY IT WAS "FOR HUMANITY."
THE GIRLS HAVE TRIED TRICK AFTER TRICK TO GET US IN THE MOOD.
IF WE DO GO ALONG WITH THEM AND HAVE SEX...
THEN WE'LL HAVE SERVED OUR PURPOSE AND MOST LIKELY BE KILLED.
WE CAN AT LEAST SAY WE HAVE SEEN A MAN LIKE US GET SHOT TO DEATH.
THERE ALSO HAS TO BE A REASON THEY HAVEN'T USED THOSE WEAPONS TO THREATEN US TO FOLLOW THEIR ORDERS.
SO MAYBE... IF WE'RE NOT INTO IT, THEN THEIR PLAN DOESN'T WORK FOR SOME REASON?

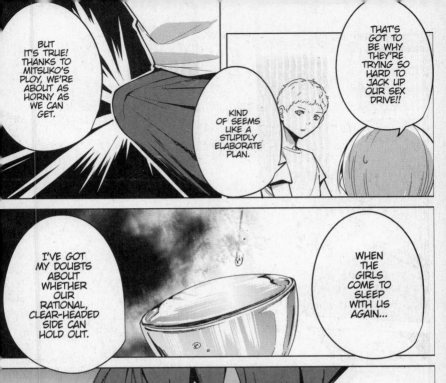

BUT IT'S TRUE! THANKS TO MITSUKO'S PLOY, WE'RE ABOUT AS HORNY AS WE CAN GET.

KIND OF SEEMS LIKE A STUPIDLY ELABORATE PLAN.

THAT'S GOT TO BE WHY THEY'RE TRYING SO HARD TO JACK UP OUR SEX DRIVE!!

I'VE GOT MY DOUBTS ABOUT WHETHER OUR RATIONAL, CLEAR-HEADED SIDE CAN HOLD OUT.

WHEN THE GIRLS COME TO SLEEP WITH US AGAIN...

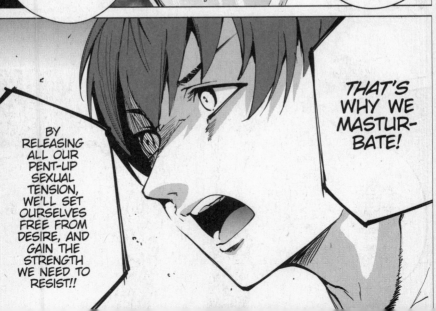

BY RELEASING ALL OUR PENT-UP SEXUAL TENSION, WE'LL SET OURSELVES FREE FROM DESIRE, AND GAIN THE STRENGTH WE NEED TO RESIST!!

THAT'S WHY WE MASTUR-BATE!

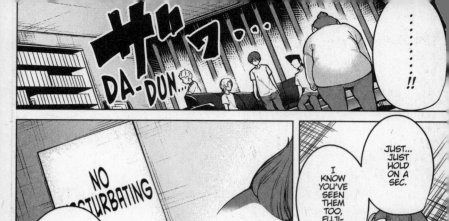

ザッ ザワ... DA-DUN...

．．．．
．．．．
!!

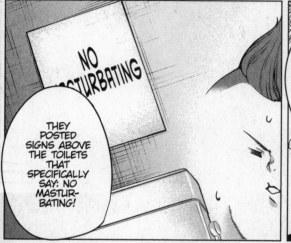

NO MASTURBATING

THEY POSTED SIGNS ABOVE THE TOILETS THAT SPECIFICALLY SAY: NO MASTUR-BATING!

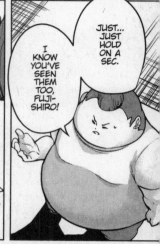

JUST... JUST HOLD ON A SEC.

I KNOW YOU'VE SEEN THEM TOO, FUJI-SHIRO!

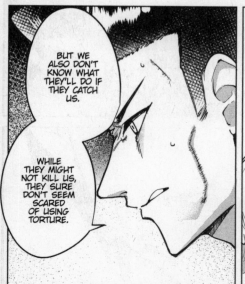

BUT WE ALSO DON'T KNOW WHAT THEY'LL DO IF THEY CATCH US.

WHILE THEY MIGHT NOT KILL US, THEY SURE DON'T SEEM SCARED OF USING TORTURE.

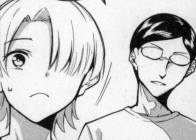

IF OUR HYPOTHESIS THAT THE GIRLS WANT TO HAVE SEX WITH US AT ANY COST IS TRUE...

THEN THEY WOULDN'T KILL US OVER SMALL VIOLATIONS OF THE RULES. ...PROBABLY.

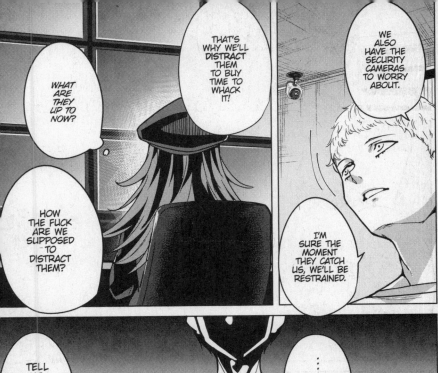

WHAT ARE THEY UP TO NOW?

THAT'S WHY WE'LL DISTRACT THEM TO BUY TIME TO WHACK IT!

WE ALSO HAVE THE SECURITY CAMERAS TO WORRY ABOUT.

HOW THE FUCK ARE WE SUPPOSED TO DISTRACT THEM?

I'M SURE THE MOMENT THEY CATCH US, WE'LL BE RESTRAINED.

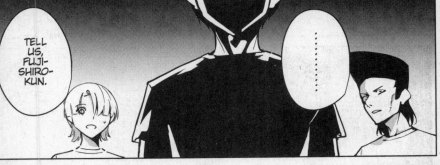

TELL US, FUJI-SHIRO-KUN.

. . . . . .

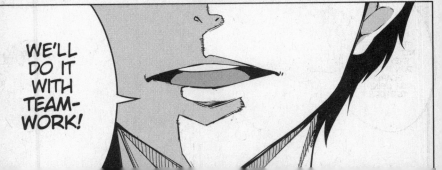

WE'LL DO IT WITH TEAM-WORK!

IF WE ALL WORK TOGETHER...
WE CAN PULL THROUGH THESE DIFFICULT TIMES...AND MASTURBATE!!
WE HAVE UNTIL TONIGHT. UNTIL THE GIRLS COME TO OUR BEDS.
JUST STANDING AROUND ISN'T GOING TO MAKE US ANY LESS HORNY!
MASTUR-BATION IS OUR ONLY OPTION!!

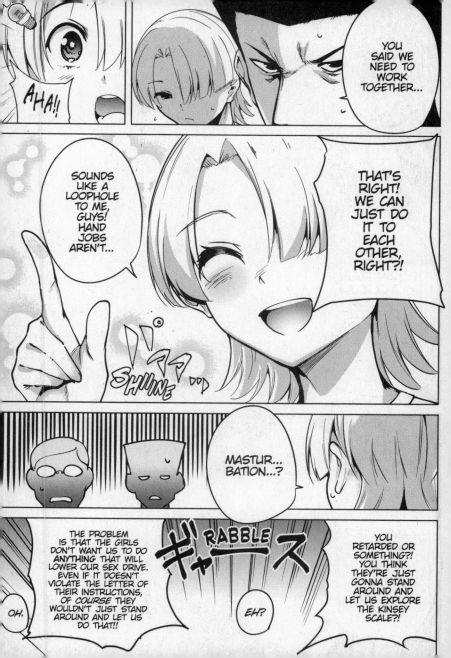

AHA!!

YOU SAID WE NEED TO WORK TOGETHER...

SOUNDS LIKE A LOOPHOLE TO ME, GUYS! HAND JOBS AREN'T...

THAT'S RIGHT! WE CAN JUST DO IT TO EACH OTHER, RIGHT?!

SHIIINE

MASTUR... BATION...?

RABBLE

THE PROBLEM IS THAT THE GIRLS DON'T WANT US TO DO ANYTHING THAT WILL LOWER OUR SEX DRIVE. EVEN IF IT DOESN'T VIOLATE THE LETTER OF THEIR INSTRUCTIONS, OF COURSE THEY WOULDN'T JUST STAND AROUND AND LET US DO THAT!!

OH.

EH?

YOU RETARDED OR SOMETHING?! YOU THINK THEY'RE JUST GONNA STAND AROUND AND LET US EXPLORE THE KINSEY SCALE?!

しゅん…
SLUMP...
WELL... I TRIED...
WELL, NO SENSE CHANGING TOPICS NOW.
YOU DO HAVE SOME KIND OF PLAN, RIGHT?
YEAH.
Listen...
You must hide... and mastur-bate.
FWSH...
ボッ
Huh?!
Our surveil-lance is good...
but it isn't perfect. When you find a chance, slip away.

In a way where we won't catch you...
You need... to masturbate.
BLUUUSH...
カアァ…ッ
I...I'm sorry, could you say that again?
Our surveillance is tight, but--
No, the thing before that.
SHE LOOKED SO EMBARRASSED TO SAY IT.
I DIDN'T MISHEAR HER AFTER ALL!
PAY ATTENTION! SHE'S BEING TOTALLY SERIOUS ABOUT THIS!
Okay, but I'm only going to say it once. Got it?
I understand... Go on.
SAYAKA-CHAN IS CUTE EVEN WHEN SHE'S EMBARRASSED.

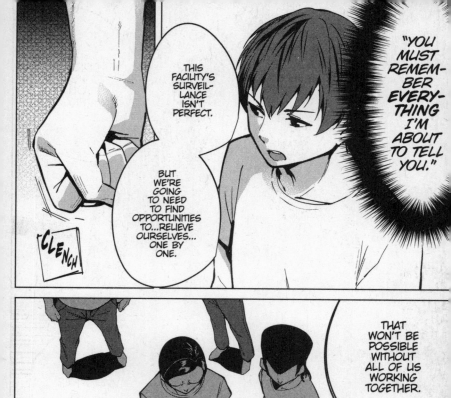

"YOU MUST REMEMBER EVERYTHING I'M ABOUT TO TELL YOU."

THIS FACILITY'S SURVEILLANCE ISN'T PERFECT.

BUT WE'RE GOING TO NEED TO FIND OPPORTUNITIES TO...RELIEVE OURSELVES... ONE BY ONE.

CLENCH

THAT WON'T BE POSSIBLE WITHOUT ALL OF US WORKING TOGETHER.

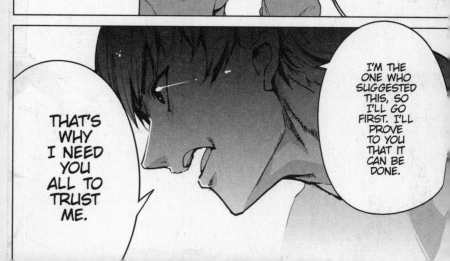

THAT'S WHY I NEED YOU ALL TO TRUST ME.

I'M THE ONE WHO SUGGESTED THIS, SO I'LL GO FIRST. I'LL PROVE TO YOU THAT IT CAN BE DONE.

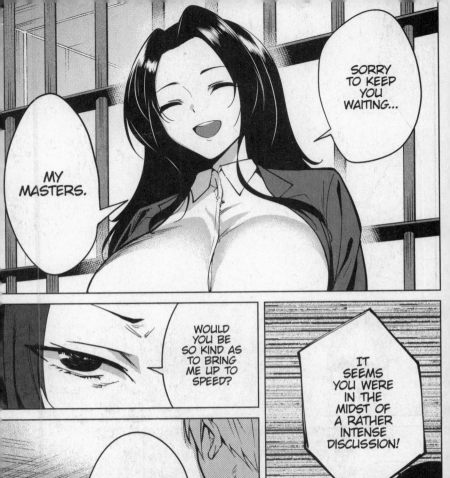

SORRY TO KEEP YOU WAITING...

MY MASTERS.

WOULD YOU BE SO KIND AS TO BRING ME UP TO SPEED?

IT SEEMS YOU WERE IN THE MIDST OF A RATHER INTENSE DISCUSSION!

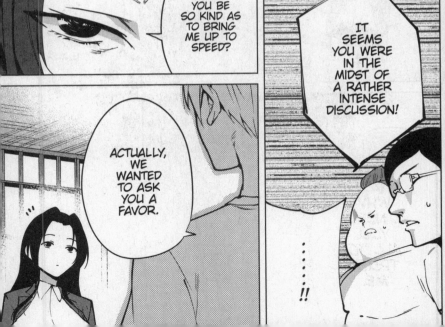

ACTUALLY, WE WANTED TO ASK YOU A FAVOR.

. . . . . .

!!

WE WANT TO EAT YAKINIKU FOR BREAK-FAST...
AND WE WANT TO EAT IT OFF YOUR NAKED BODY.

COME AGAIN?
FOURTEEN HOURS UNTIL NIGHTFALL.

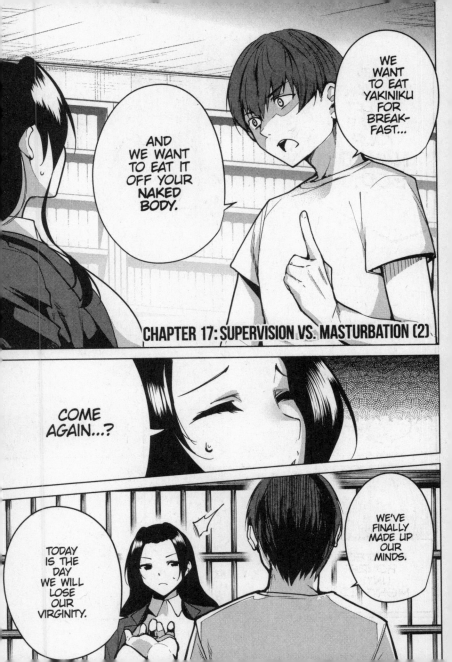

WE WANT TO EAT YAKINIKU FOR BREAKFAST...

AND WE WANT TO EAT IT OFF YOUR NAKED BODY.

CHAPTER 17: SUPERVISION VS. MASTURBATION (2)

COME AGAIN...?

WE'VE FINALLY MADE UP OUR MINDS.

TODAY IS THE DAY WE WILL LOSE OUR VIRGINITY.

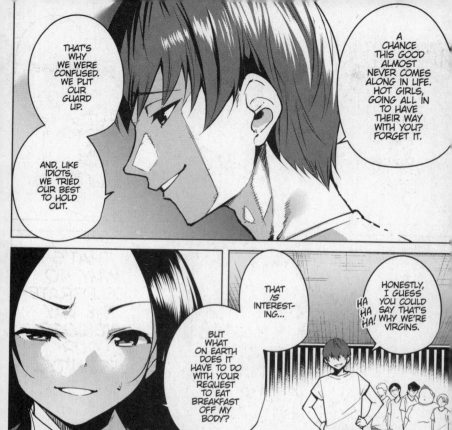

A CHANCE THIS GOOD ALMOST NEVER COMES ALONG IN LIFE. HOT GIRLS, GOING ALL IN TO HAVE THEIR WAY WITH YOU? FORGET IT.

THAT'S WHY WE WERE CONFUSED. WE PUT OUR GUARD UP.

AND, LIKE IDIOTS, WE TRIED OUR BEST TO HOLD OUT.

HONESTLY, I GUESS YOU COULD SAY THAT'S WHY WE'RE VIRGINS.

HA HA HA!

THAT IS INTERESTING...

BUT WHAT ON EARTH DOES IT HAVE TO DO WITH YOUR REQUEST TO EAT BREAKFAST OFF MY BODY?

I GUESS YOU COULD SAY IT'S A LIFELONG FANTASY OF MINE.

BESIDES...
WE ALL HAVE OUR REASONS FOR STAYING VIRGINS ALL THIS TIME.
IF WE'RE GOING TO THROW THAT AWAY, WE WANT TO AT LEAST MAKE THE OCCASION SPECIAL.
THAT'S WHY, TO CELEBRATE THE DAY WE LOSE OUR VIRGINITY...
WE WANT TO ENJOY THE WHOLE DAY...AND EAT OFF YOUR NAKED BODY!!

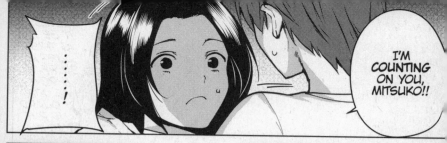

I'M COUNTING ON YOU, MITSUKO!!

...!

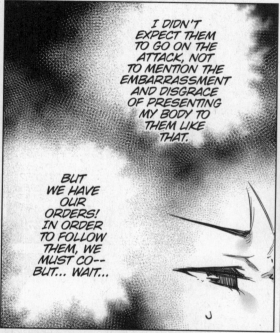

I DIDN'T EXPECT THEM TO GO ON THE ATTACK, NOT TO MENTION THE EMBARRASSMENT AND DISGRACE OF PRESENTING MY BODY TO THEM LIKE THAT.

BUT WE HAVE OUR ORDERS! IN ORDER TO FOLLOW THEM, WE MUST CO-- BUT... WAIT...

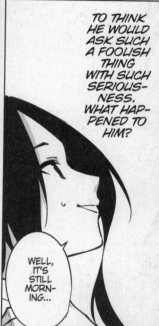

TO THINK HE WOULD ASK SUCH A FOOLISH THING WITH SUCH SERIOUSNESS. WHAT HAPPENED TO HIM?

WELL, IT'S STILL MORNING...

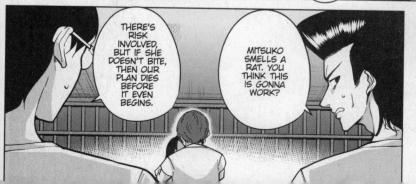

THERE'S RISK INVOLVED, BUT IF SHE DOESN'T BITE, THEN OUR PLAN DIES BEFORE IT EVEN BEGINS.

MITSUKO SMELLS A RAT. YOU THINK THIS IS GONNA WORK?

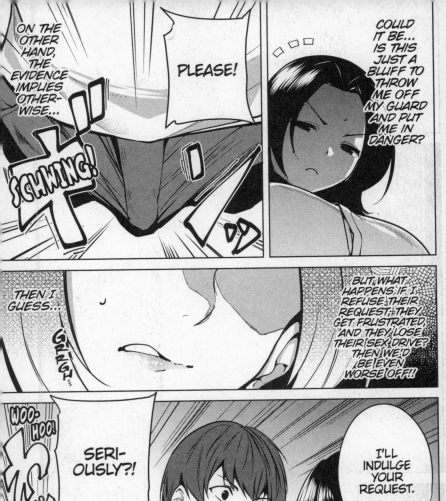

ON THE OTHER HAND, THE EVIDENCE IMPLIES OTHER-WISE...

PLEASE!

COULD IT BE... IS THIS JUST A BLUFF TO THROW ME OFF MY GUARD AND PUT ME IN DANGER?

SCHWING!

THEN I GUESS...

GRGH...

BUT, WHAT HAPPENS IF I REFUSE THEIR REQUEST, THEY GET FRUSTRATED, AND THEY LOSE THEIR SEX DRIVE? THEN WE'D BE EVEN WORSE OFF!!

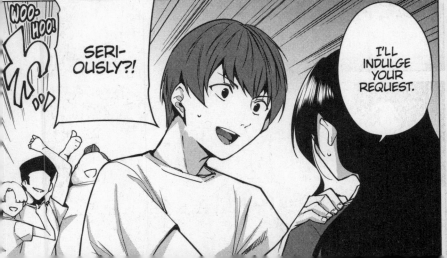

WOO-HOO!

SERI-OUSLY?!

I'LL INDULGE YOUR REQUEST.

NICE! MY FANTASY COMES TRUE, BABY!!
THANKS, MITSUKO! YOU REALLY DO GET ME!!
I GUESS GOOD THINGS COME TO THOSE WHO ASK!
PHEW...
WILL EVERYONE ELSE BE PARTAKING?
YOU BET YOUR ASS.
THEN I WILL BEGIN THE PREPARATIONS. PLEASE GIVE ME A SHORT WHILE.
NICE! IT'S JUST AS SAYAKA-CHAN SAID.
SMIRK
For the most part...
If you say you want to have sex, you won't be refused.
Anything that gets you closer to that won't be brushed off.
Basically if you request something lewd of Mitsuko, it will most likely happen.

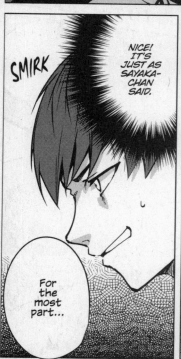

DOON
SPARKLE
BON APPETIT!

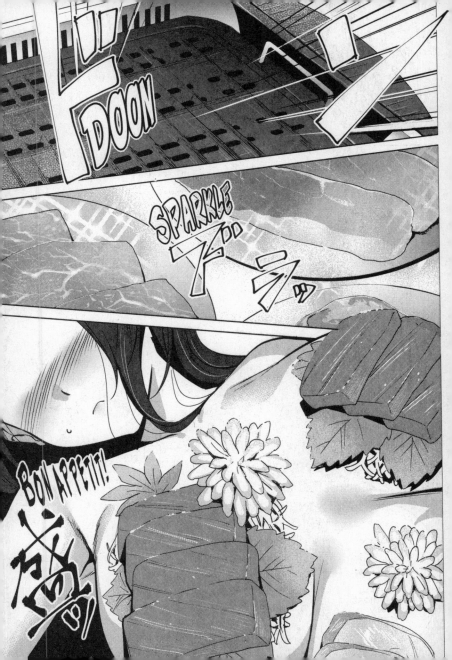

WHOOOA!!
BAAAM
GULP...
SO THIS IS WHAT IT'S LIKE TO EAT OFF A NAKED BODY!

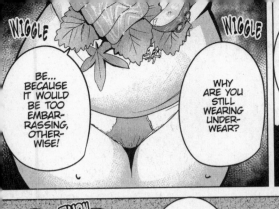

WIGGLE WIGGLE

BE... BECAUSE IT WOULD BE TOO EMBAR-RASSING, OTHER-WISE!

WHY ARE YOU STILL WEARING UNDER-WEAR?

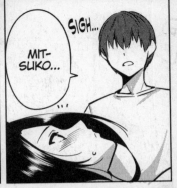

SIGH...

MIT-SUKO...

...

O-OF COURSE I CAN. JUST WHAT KIND OF PERSON DO YOU THINK I AM?

TURN

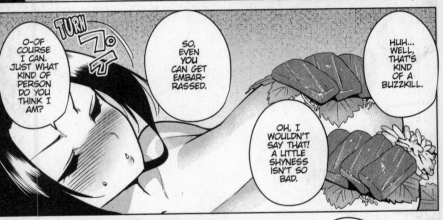

SO, EVEN YOU CAN GET EMBAR-RASSED.

HUH... WELL, THAT'S KIND OF A BUZZKILL.

OH, I WOULDN'T SAY THAT! A LITTLE SHYNESS ISN'T SO BAD.

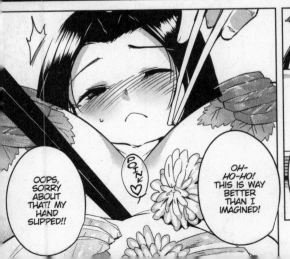

DONK

OOPS, SORRY ABOUT THAT! MY HAND SLIPPED!!

OH-HO-HO! THIS IS WAY BETTER THAN I IMAGINED!

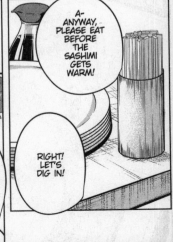

A-ANYWAY, PLEASE EAT BEFORE THE SASHIMI GETS WARM!

RIGHT! LET'S DIG IN!

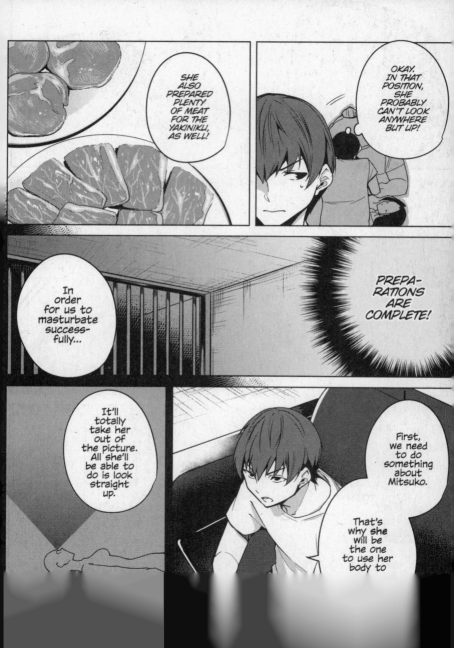

SHE ALSO PREPARED PLENTY OF MEAT FOR THE YAKINIKU, AS WELL!

OKAY. IN THAT POSITION, SHE PROBABLY CAN'T LOOK ANYWHERE BUT UP!

In order for us to masturbate successfully...

PREPARATIONS ARE COMPLETE!

It'll totally take her out of the picture. All she'll be able to do is look straight up.

First, we need to do something about Mitsuko.

That's why she will be the one to use her body to

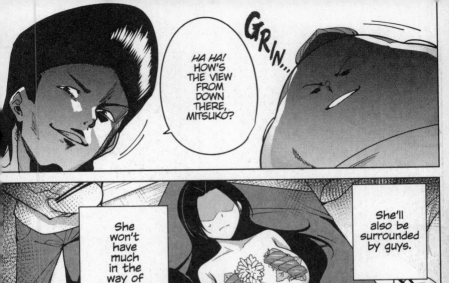

GRIN...

HA HA! HOW'S THE VIEW FROM DOWN THERE, MITSUKO?

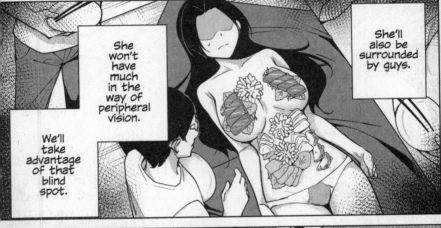

She won't have much in the way of peripheral vision.

We'll take advantage of that blind spot.

She'll also be surrounded by guys.

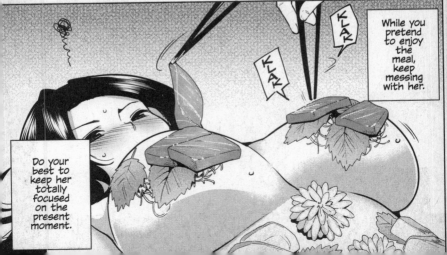

KLAK

KLAK

While you pretend to enjoy the meal, keep messing with her.

Do your best to keep her totally focused on the present moment.

I don't see a problem with Mitsuko...
but what about the security cameras?
I didn't forget about them.
Oh?
WHIRRR
In order to buy a brief time to slip by the cameras...
we'll use the yakiniku.
D... did you say yakiniku?!
Wait, you intend to make...
a smoke-screen!!
Bingo!

KAZA-MATSURI, I'LL LEAVE THE COOKIN' TO YOU.
SOUNDS GOOD!
Grill right below the camera and use the smoke to cloud the lens!
Since yakiniku is also good for energy, the girls should agree. There's hardly any chance they'd say no!
Then, while Mitsuko is disabled, and the cameras are blocked by the smoke...
HM, IS THIS FIRM THING A SCALLOP OR SOME-THING?
SQUOOSH
SQUOOSH
we can mastur-bate in total secrecy!
NGH...♡
BLUSH...
HE'S SURE ENJOYING HIMSELF...

The only problem is time.
The moment they notice something is up with the camera, they'll just send someone else.
I wonder how long it'll take them to send someone over once they do.
If I were to guess from how long it took last time, I'd say...
about two minutes.

T-two minutes?! Can we really masturbate in under two minutes?!
No matter how horny we might be, two minutes is impossible!
Shit, we had a real good plan going, too!!
That's where *I* come in.
?!
"Only" two minutes... *Heh.*
Fujishiro ...?
Two minutes will be more than enough.

DA-DUN
Because when it comes to mastur-bation...
I'm the fastest there is!!

HUH ...?

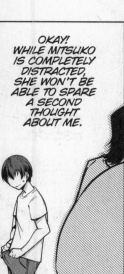

OKAY! WHILE MITSUKO IS COMPLETELY DISTRACTED, SHE WON'T BE ABLE TO SPARE A SECOND THOUGHT ABOUT ME.

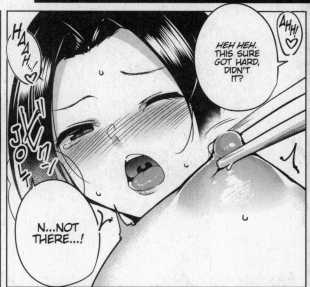

HAAH!♡

AHH!♡

HEH HEH. THIS SURE GOT HARD, DIDN'T IT?

N...NOT THERE...!

JUNX JOLT

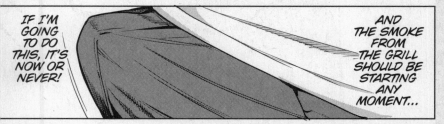

IF I'M GOING TO DO THIS, IT'S NOW OR NEVER!

AND THE SMOKE FROM THE GRILL SHOULD BE STARTING ANY MOMENT...

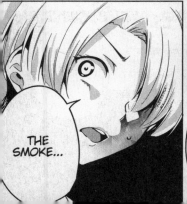

THE SMOKE...

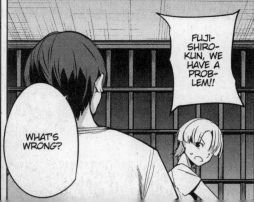

FUJI-SHIRO-KUN, WE HAVE A PROBLEM!!

WHAT'S WRONG?

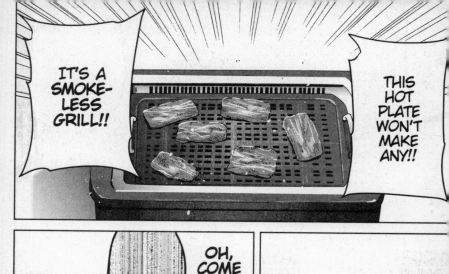

IT'S A SMOKE- LESS GRILL!!

THIS HOT PLATE WON'T MAKE ANY!!

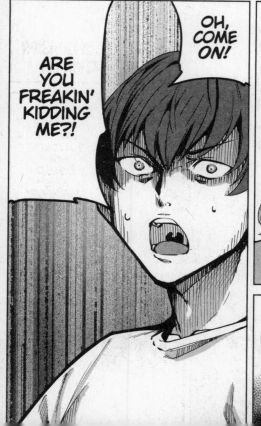

OH, COME ON!

ARE YOU FREAKIN' KIDDING ME?!

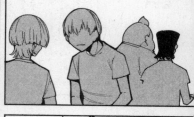

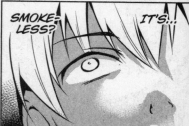

SMOKE- LESS?

IT'S...

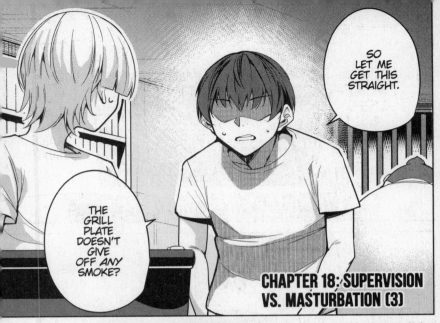

SO LET ME GET THIS STRAIGHT.

THE GRILL PLATE DOESN'T GIVE OFF ANY SMOKE?

CHAPTER 18: SUPERVISION VS. MASTURBATION (3)

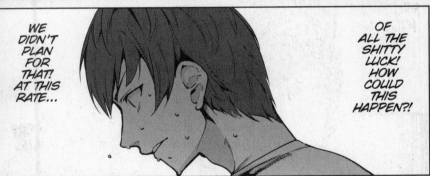

OF ALL THE SHITTY LUCK! HOW COULD THIS HAPPEN?!

WE DIDN'T PLAN FOR THAT! AT THIS RATE...

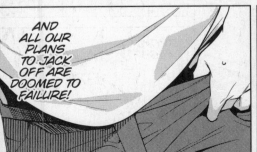

AND ALL OUR PLANS TO JACK OFF ARE DOOMED TO FAILURE!

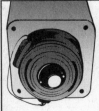

THE CAMERAS WILL SEE EVERYTHING...

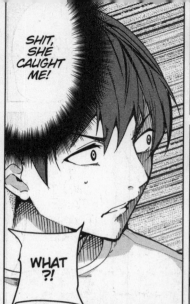

SHIT, SHE CAUGHT ME!

WHAT?!

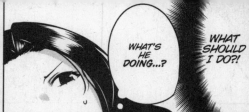

WHAT'S HE DOING...?

WHAT SHOULD I DO?!

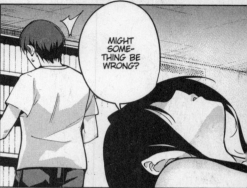

MIGHT SOMETHING BE WRONG?

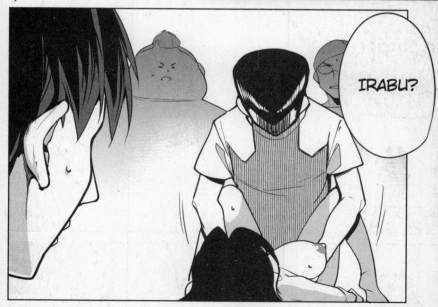

IRABU?

WH-WHAT ARE YOU--
I...
I CAN'T TAKE IT ANY-MORE!!
YANK
!!

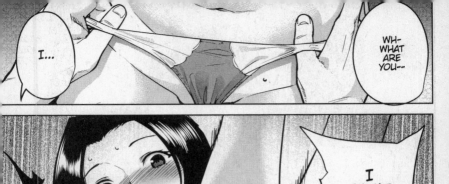

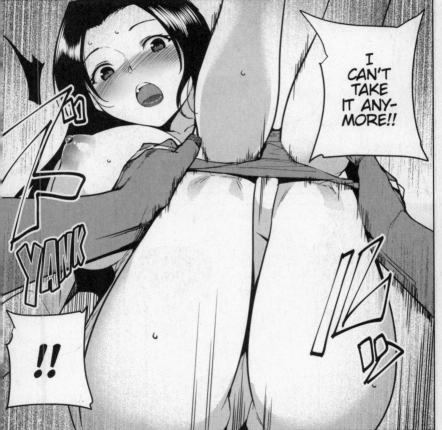

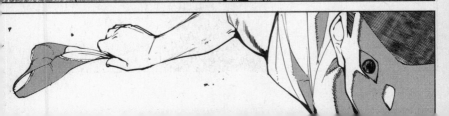

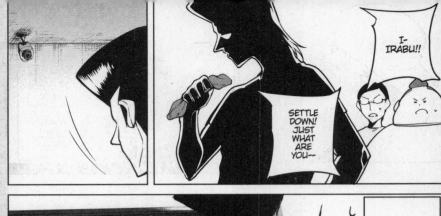

I-IRABU!!

SETTLE DOWN! JUST WHAT ARE YOU--

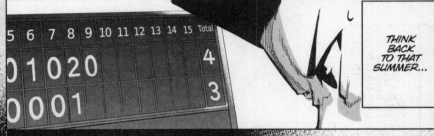

5	6	7	8	9	10	11	12	13	14	15	Total
0	1	0	2	0							4
0	0	0	1								3

THINK BACK TO THAT SUMMER...

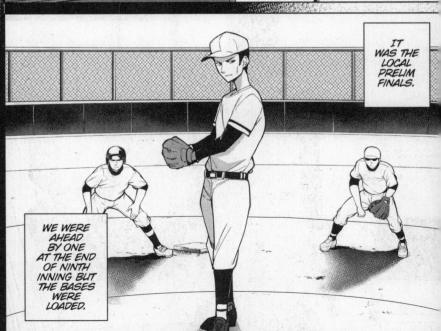

IT WAS THE LOCAL PRELIM FINALS.

WE WERE AHEAD BY ONE AT THE END OF NINTH INNING BUT THE BASES WERE LOADED.

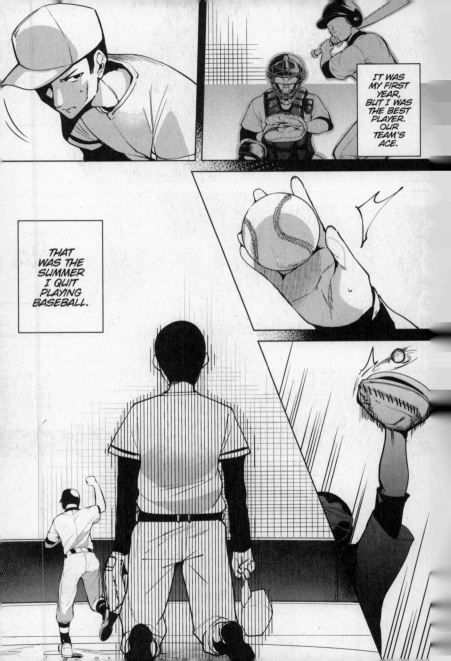

IT WAS MY FIRST YEAR, BUT I WAS THE BEST PLAYER. OUR TEAM'S ACE.

THAT WAS THE SUMMER I QUIT PLAYING BASEBALL.

BUT THIS TIME...
GRRRIP...
THIS TIME!!
ズ
CLENCH...
I WON'T MISS!!
FWOOSH

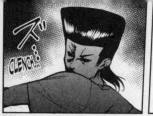

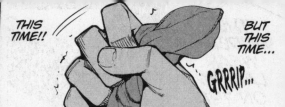

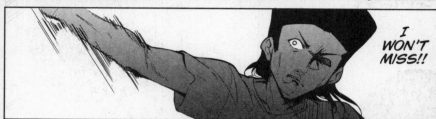

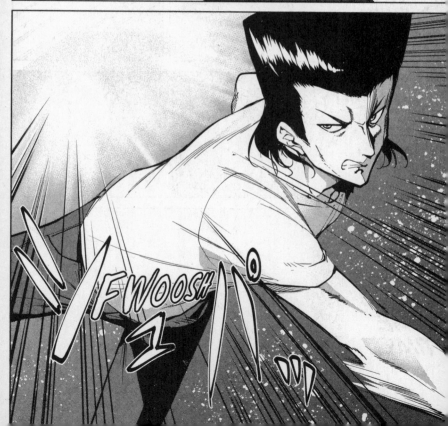

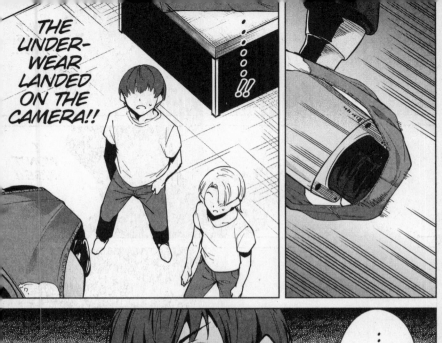

THE UNDER-WEAR LANDED ON THE CAMERA!!

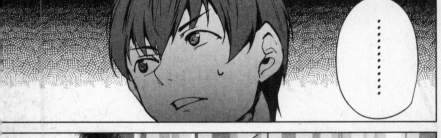

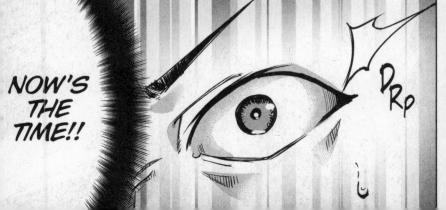

NOW'S THE TIME!!

DRp

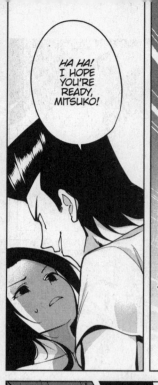

HA HA! I HOPE YOU'RE READY, MITSUKO!

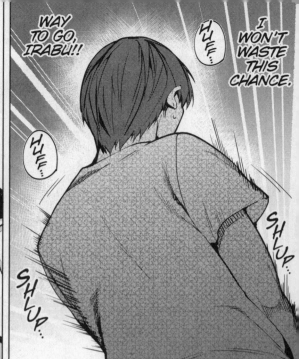

WAY TO GO, IRABU!!

HUFF...

HUFF...

I WON'T WASTE THIS CHANCE.

SHUP...

SHUP...

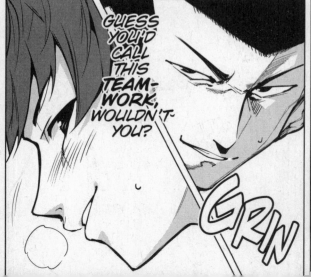

GUESS YOU'D CALL THIS TEAM-WORK, WOULDN'T YOU?

GRIN

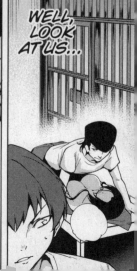

WELL, LOOK AT US...

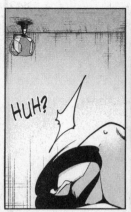

HUH?

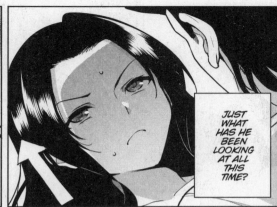

JUST WHAT HAS HE BEEN LOOKING AT ALL THIS TIME?

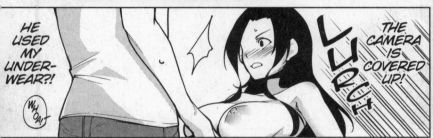

HE USED MY UNDER-WEAR?!

WHOA!

THE CAMERA IS COVERED UP!

LURU

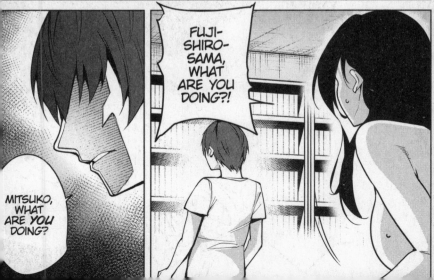

FUJI-SHIRO-SAMA, WHAT ARE YOU DOING?!

MITSUKO, WHAT ARE *YOU* DOING?

PHEW...
WE AREN'T FINISHED EATING YET.
HE DID IT!!
I THOUGHT WE WERE JUST GETTING STARTED.
HA. LOOKS LIKE I'M JUST NOT FEELING IT ANYMORE.

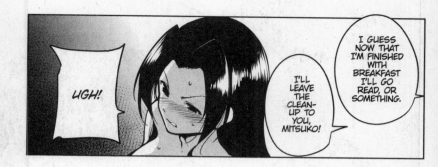

UGH!

I'LL LEAVE THE CLEAN-UP TO YOU, MITSUKO!

I GUESS NOW THAT I'M FINISHED WITH BREAKFAST I'LL GO READ, OR SOMETHING.

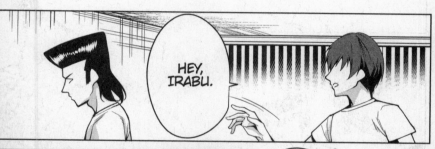

HEY, IRABU.

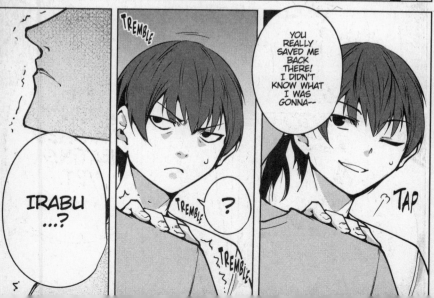

TREMBLE

YOU REALLY SAVED ME BACK THERE! I DIDN'T KNOW WHAT I WAS GONNA--

IRABU...?

TREMBLE

?

TREMBLE

TAP

JOLT...
TREMBLE
WHAT'S WRONG?!
HEH HEH. DON'T WORRY.
I JUST REMEMBERED HOW I FELT BACK THERE, AND, WELL...
LOOKS LIKE...
I CAME.

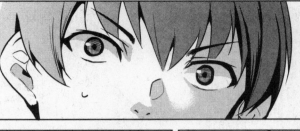

YOU GOT OFF USING NOTHING BUT THE POWER OF YOUR MIND?!

WHAT WAS THAT?!

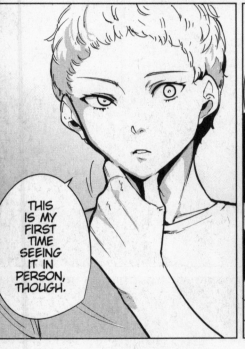

THIS IS MY FIRST TIME SEEING IT IN PERSON, THOUGH.

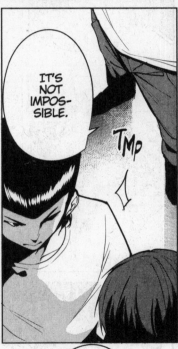

IT'S NOT IMPOSSIBLE.

TMP

A WET DREAM?!

IT WAS MOST LIKELY A WET DREAM.

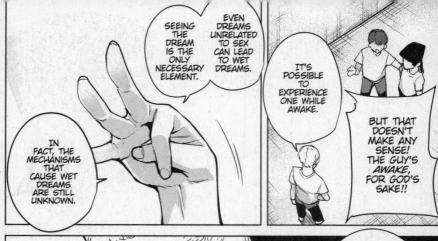

SEEING THE DREAM IS THE ONLY NECESSARY ELEMENT.

EVEN DREAMS UNRELATED TO SEX CAN LEAD TO WET DREAMS.

IT'S POSSIBLE TO EXPERIENCE ONE WHILE AWAKE.

BUT THAT DOESN'T MAKE ANY SENSE! THE GUY'S AWAKE, FOR GOD'S SAKE!!

IN FACT, THE MECHANISMS THAT CAUSE WET DREAMS ARE STILL UNKNOWN.

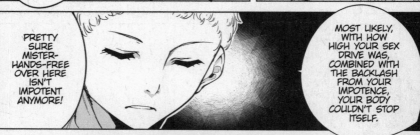

PRETTY SURE MISTER-HANDS-FREE OVER HERE ISN'T IMPOTENT ANYMORE!

MOST LIKELY, WITH HOW HIGH YOUR SEX DRIVE WAS, COMBINED WITH THE BACKLASH FROM YOUR IMPOTENCE, YOUR BODY COULDN'T STOP ITSELF.

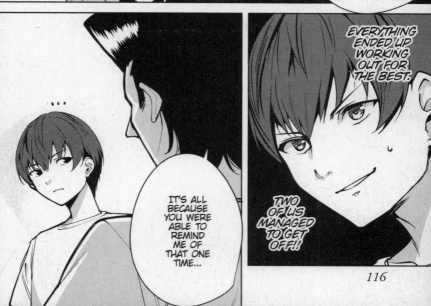

...

IT'S ALL BECAUSE YOU WERE ABLE TO REMIND ME OF THAT ONE TIME...

EVERYTHING ENDED UP WORKING OUT FOR THE BEST.

TWO OF US MANAGED TO GET OFF!!

THANKS, FUJISHIRO!
WHEW...
HIGH
FIVE

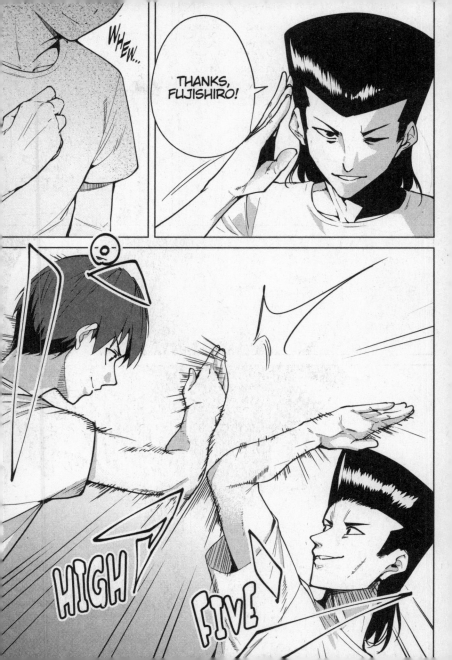

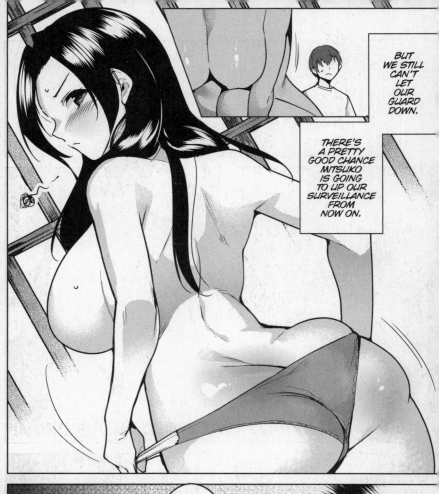

BUT WE STILL CAN'T LET OUR GUARD DOWN.

THERE'S A PRETTY GOOD CHANCE MITSUKO IS GOING TO UP OUR SURVEILLANCE FROM NOW ON.

TWELVE HOURS UNTIL NIGHTFALL.

I WONDER IF THEY GAVE US ANY EXTRA UNDIES...

ONLY FOUR LEFT. IF WE CAN JUST GET EVERYONE TO SAFELY MASTURBATE, WE'LL HAVE THE UPPER HAND!!

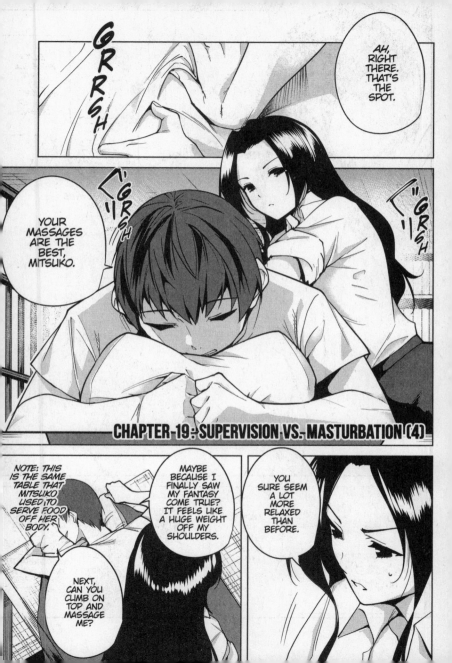

CHAPTER 19: SUPERVISION VS. MASTURBATION (4)

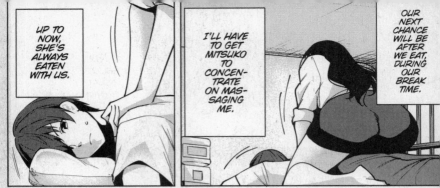

UP TO NOW, SHE'S ALWAYS EATEN WITH US.

I'LL HAVE TO GET MITSUKO TO CONCENTRATE ON MASSAGING ME.

OUR NEXT CHANCE WILL BE AFTER WE EAT, DURING OUR BREAK TIME.

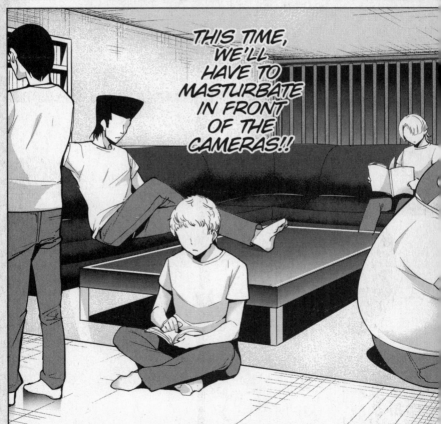

THIS TIME, WE'LL HAVE TO MASTURBATE IN FRONT OF THE CAMERAS!!

The second time we do it...
we won't be touching the camera.
?!
After our first stunt with the panties...
the girls will undoubtedly be on guard. We won't be able to use the same technique twice.
But then... how are we going to do it?
There aren't any spots where the camera doesn't reach in this cell.
If there aren't any spots...
We will just have to make some!

EVERYONE IS PLACED PERFECTLY TO LOOK LIKE THEY'RE JUST GOING ABOUT THEIR OWN THING.
BUT IN REALITY...
DA-DUN
WE'RE ALL WORKING TOGETHER TO ACHIEVE A SINGLE GOAL.
HIDE KAZA-MATSURI'S CROTCH!!

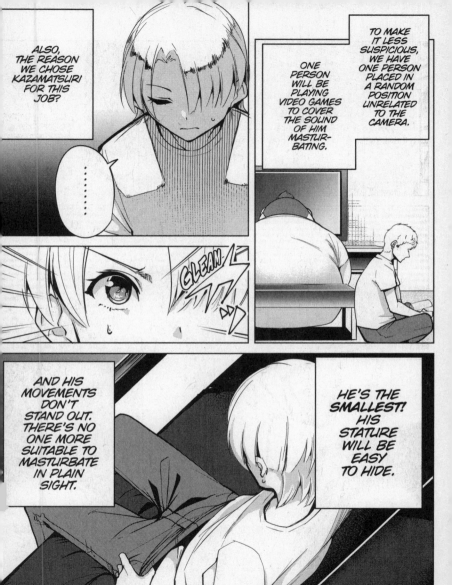

ALSO, THE REASON WE CHOSE KAZAMATSURI FOR THIS JOB?

. . . .

ONE PERSON WILL BE PLAYING VIDEO GAMES TO COVER THE SOUND OF HIM MASTUR-BATING.

TO MAKE IT LESS SUSPICIOUS, WE HAVE ONE PERSON PLACED IN A RANDOM POSITION UNRELATED TO THE CAMERA.

GLEAM

AND HIS MOVEMENTS DON'T STAND OUT. THERE'S NO ONE MORE SUITABLE TO MASTURBATE IN PLAIN SIGHT.

HE'S THE SMALLEST! HIS STATURE WILL BE EASY TO HIDE.

123

HOLD YOUR CHEST HIGH, KAZA-MATSURI!
HUFF...
YOUR SMALL-NESS IS YOUR GREATEST WEAPON!!
HUFF...
YOU'RE NOT ALONE!
SMIRK
HUFF...
BA-DUM

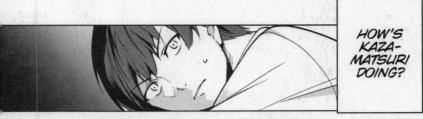

HOW'S KAZA-MATSURI DOING?

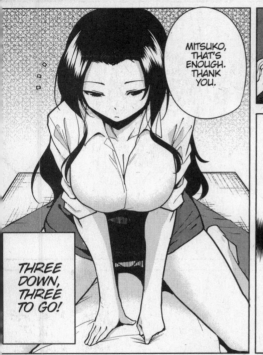

MITSUKO, THAT'S ENOUGH. THANK YOU.

THREE DOWN, THREE TO GO!

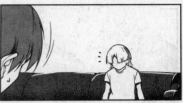

NICE!!

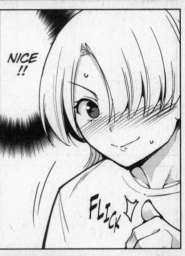

FLICK

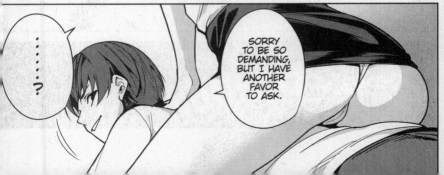

......?

SORRY TO BE SO DEMANDING, BUT I HAVE ANOTHER FAVOR TO ASK.

COULD YOU TEACH US HOW TO DO THE ARMY CRAWL?
MAY I ASK... WHY?
WE'RE ALL USED TO HAVING DAILY WORKOUTS NOW.
I WAS HOPING WE COULD TRY SOMETHING A LITTLE MORE PRACTICAL.

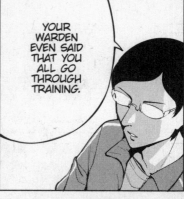

YOUR WARDEN EVEN SAID THAT YOU ALL GO THROUGH TRAINING.

PLEASE, DON'T MISUNDERSTAND. WE'RE NOT TRYING TO BE DIFFICULT.

····· !!

WE WERE JUST HOPING TO DO SOMETHING MORE PRACTICAL.

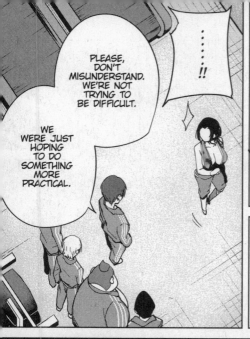

IF YOU HAVE KNOWLEDGE OF ARMY-STYLE MARTIAL ARTS, THEN YOU SHOULD KNOW HOW TO ARMY CRAWL.

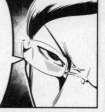

WE ALSO WANT TO CONDITION OUR HIPS FOR USE WHILE LYING DOWN.

WE ARE VIRGINS, AFTER ALL. IF WE DON'T PRACTICE, THEN WE MIGHT BE TOO WEAK TO USE THEM FOR THE REAL THING.

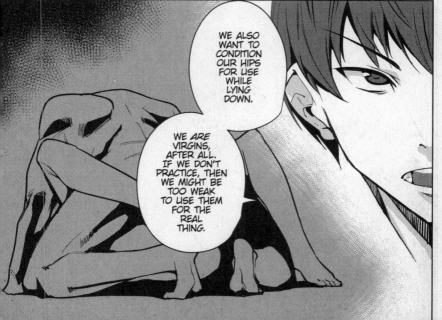

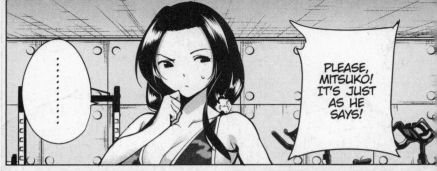

PLEASE, MITSUKO! IT'S JUST AS HE SAYS!

・・・・・・

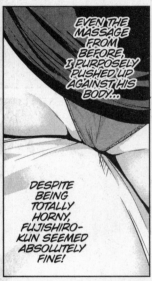

EVEN THE MASSAGE FROM BEFORE, I PURPOSELY PUSHED UP AGAINST HIS BODY...

DESPITE BEING TOTALLY HORNY, FUJISHIRO-KUN SEEMED ABSOLUTELY FINE!

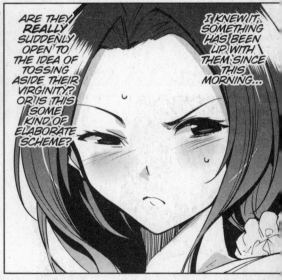

ARE THEY **REALLY** SUDDENLY OPEN TO THE IDEA OF TOSSING ASIDE THEIR VIRGINITY? OR IS THIS SOME KIND OF ELABORATE SCHEME?

I KNEW IT, SOMETHING HAS BEEN UP WITH THEM SINCE THIS MORNING...

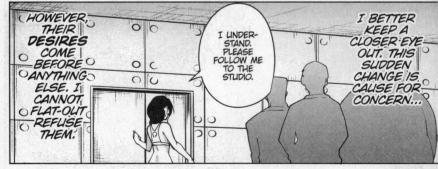

HOWEVER, THEIR **DESIRES** COME BEFORE ANYTHING ELSE. I CANNOT FLAT-OUT REFUSE THEM.

I UNDER-STAND. PLEASE FOLLOW ME TO THE STUDIO.

I BETTER KEEP A CLOSER EYE OUT. THIS SUDDEN CHANGE IS CAUSE FOR CONCERN...

HUFF..!
AHN...
HUFF..!
HAAH...
AAH...

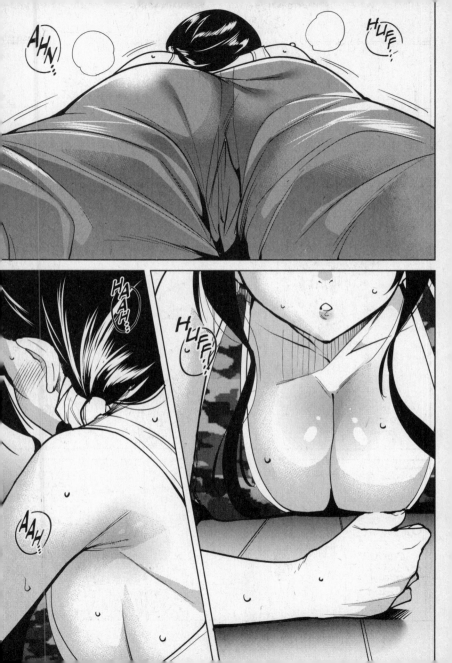

SO, YOU SHOULD MOVE LIKE THIS.
WE WILL NOW DO A LAP AROUND THE STUDIO, SO PLEASE FOLLOW BEHIND ME.
WHOA! HER MOVES LOOK LEGIT!
TH-THIS IS A LOT MORE DIFFICULT THAN I THOUGHT!
AND MY ELBOWS HURT! IS THERE SOME KIND OF GUARD FOR THAT?!
....

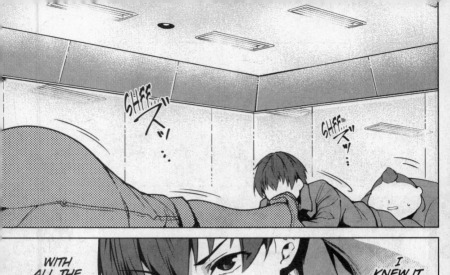

SHFF

SHFF

WITH ALL THE MIRRORS IN THE STUDIO, SHE CAN EASILY SEE WHAT WE'RE ALL DOING!

I KNEW IT. MITSUKO HAS HER GUARD UP.

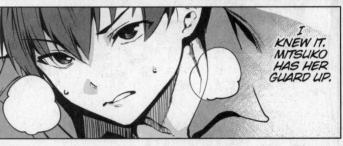

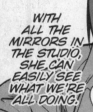

SMIRK

THAT'S RIGHT...

BUT, IT LOOKS LIKE SHE HASN'T NOTICED.

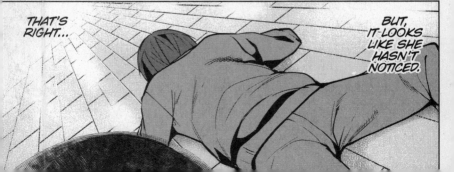

THE MASTURBATION HAS ALREADY STARTED!!

FWOOO

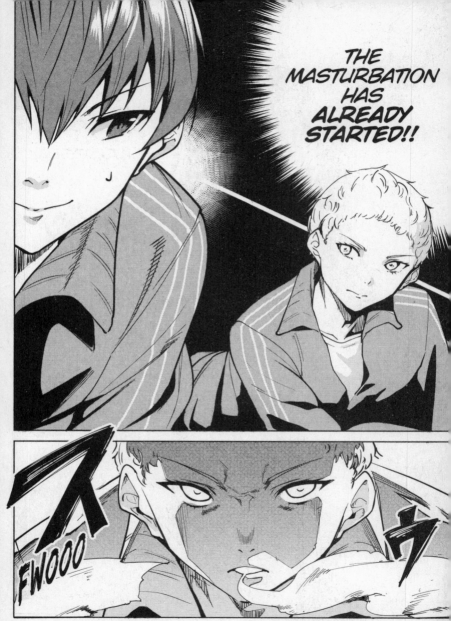

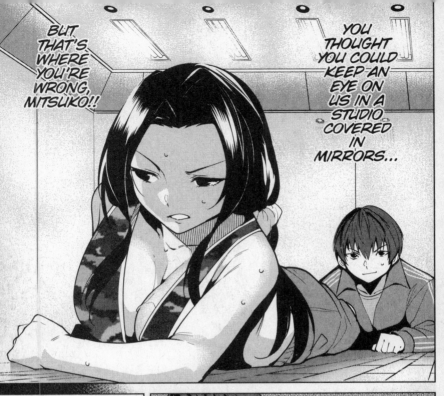

BUT, THAT'S WHERE YOU'RE WRONG, MITSUKO!!

YOU THOUGHT YOU COULD KEEP AN EYE ON US IN A STUDIO COVERED IN MIRRORS...

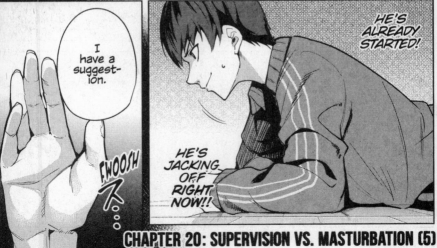

I have a suggestion.

FWOOSH

HE'S ALREADY STARTED!

HE'S JACKING OFF RIGHT NOW!!

CHAPTER 20: SUPERVISION VS. MASTURBATION (5)

What is it?
I don't need my hands to get off.
What?!
I call it the hands-free.
I can use the friction from the floor and the lower half of my body to mastur-bate.
If we're trying to get off without being caught, it might come in handy.
......
AHA...!
Perfect! Let's go with that plan!

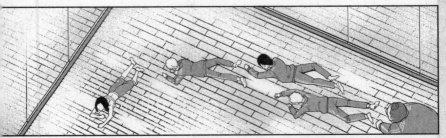

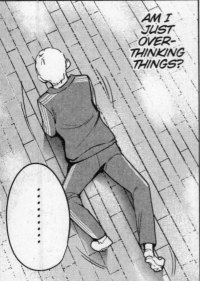

AM I JUST OVER-THINKING THINGS?

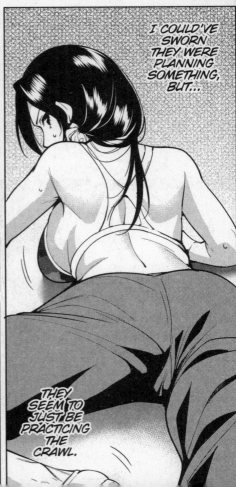

I COULD'VE SWORN THEY WERE PLANNING SOMETHING, BUT...

THEY SEEM TO JUST BE PRACTICING THE CRAWL.

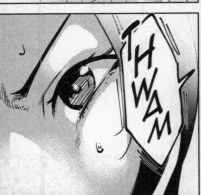

THWAM

?!
ARE YOU OKAY?!
....
YEAH, I JUST PUSHED MYSELF A LITTLE TOO HARD.
FWIP
I CAN KEEP GOING.
PLEASE, CONTINUE.

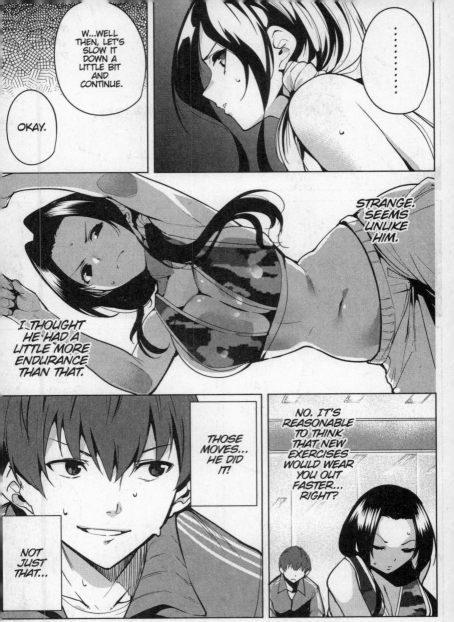

W...WELL THEN, LET'S SLOW IT DOWN A LITTLE BIT AND CONTINUE.

....

OKAY.

STRANGE. SEEMS UNLIKE HIM.

I THOUGHT HE HAD A LITTLE MORE ENDURANCE THAN THAT.

THOSE MOVES... HE DID IT!

NOT JUST THAT...

NO. IT'S REASONABLE TO THINK THAT NEW EXERCISES WOULD WEAR YOU OUT FASTER... RIGHT?

HE'S GOING FOR ROUND TWO!
ZWOOH...
HE'S TRYING TO SHOOT A DOUBLE LOAD!!
WOW, TALK ABOUT COMMIT-MENT!!
IN THE END, HE USED THE CRAWL...
TO GET OFF NO LESS THAN FIVE TIMES.

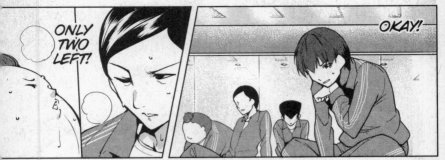

ONLY
TWO
LEFT!

OKAY!

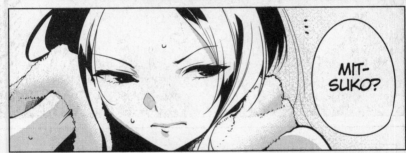

MIT-
SUKO?

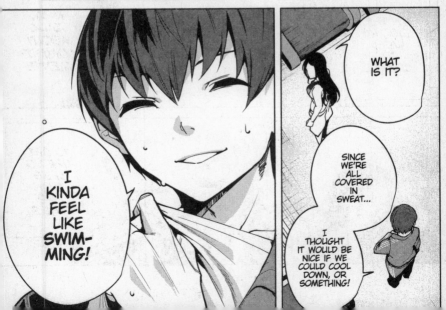

WHAT
IS IT?

SINCE
WE'RE
ALL
COVERED
IN
SWEAT...

I KINDA
FEEL
LIKE
SWIM-
MING!

I
THOUGHT
IT WOULD BE
NICE IF WE
COULD COOL
DOWN, OR
SOMETHING!

NICE!!
I CAN'T BELIEVE THIS PLACE ACTUALLY HAS A POOL!
THERE ARE CAMERAS, BUT THEY CAN'T SEE UNDER THE WATER.
WHILE MITSUKO IS DISTRACTED, WE SHOULD BE ABLE TO HAVE EVERYONE ELSE GET OFF.

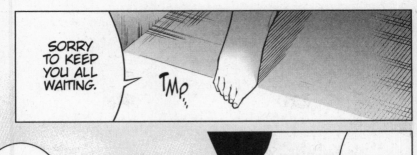

SORRY TO KEEP YOU ALL WAITING.

TMP...

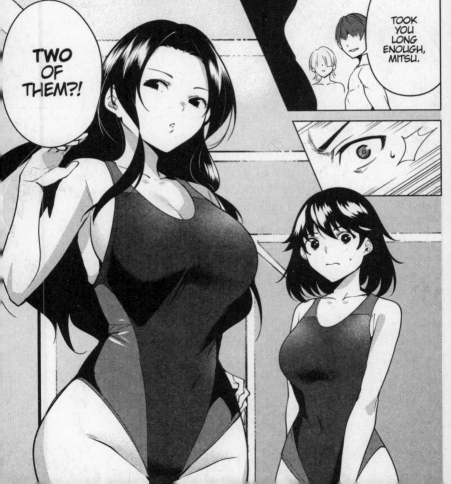

TWO OF THEM?!

TOOK YOU LONG ENOUGH, MITSU.

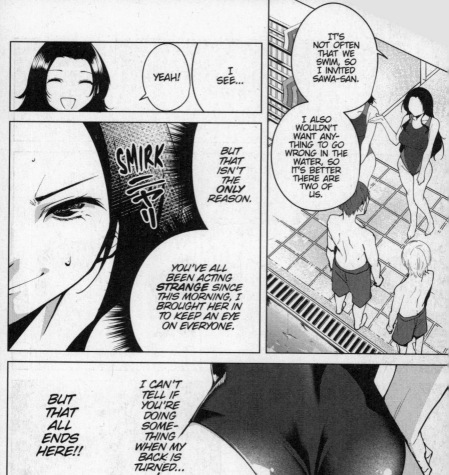

YEAH!

I SEE...

IT'S NOT OFTEN THAT WE SWIM, SO I INVITED SAWA-SAN.

I ALSO WOULDN'T WANT ANYTHING TO GO WRONG IN THE WATER, SO IT'S BETTER THERE ARE TWO OF US.

SMIRK

BUT THAT ISN'T THE ONLY REASON.

YOU'VE ALL BEEN ACTING *STRANGE* SINCE THIS MORNING, I BROUGHT HER IN TO KEEP AN EYE ON EVERYONE.

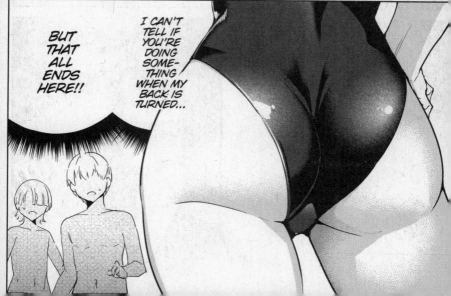

BUT THAT ALL ENDS HERE!!

I CAN'T TELL IF YOU'RE DOING SOMETHING WHEN MY BACK IS TURNED...

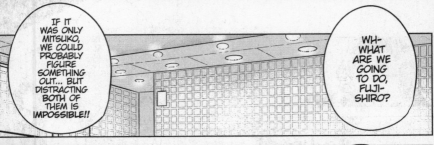

IF IT WAS ONLY MITSUKO, WE COULD PROBABLY FIGURE SOMETHING OUT... BUT DISTRACTING BOTH OF THEM IS IMPOSSIBLE!!

WH-WHAT ARE WE GOING TO DO, FUJI-SHIRO?

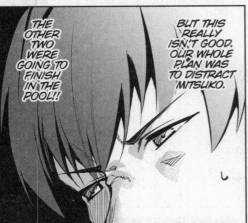

THE OTHER TWO WERE GOING TO FINISH IN THE POOL!!

BUT THIS REALLY ISN'T GOOD. OUR WHOLE PLAN WAS TO DISTRACT MITSUKO.

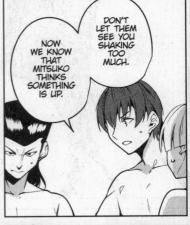

NOW WE KNOW THAT MITSUKO THINKS SOMETHING IS UP.

DON'T LET THEM SEE YOU SHAKING TOO MUCH.

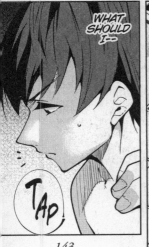

WHAT SHOULD I--

TAP

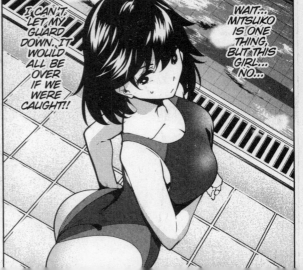

I CAN'T LET MY GUARD DOWN. IT WOULD ALL BE OVER IF WE WERE CAUGHT!!

WAIT... MITSUKO IS ONE THING, BUT THIS GIRL... NO...

143

LEAVE THIS TO ME.
NOD
OGA-WARA?
LOOKS TO ME...
DUNNN
LIKE MY TIME HAS FINALLY COME!!

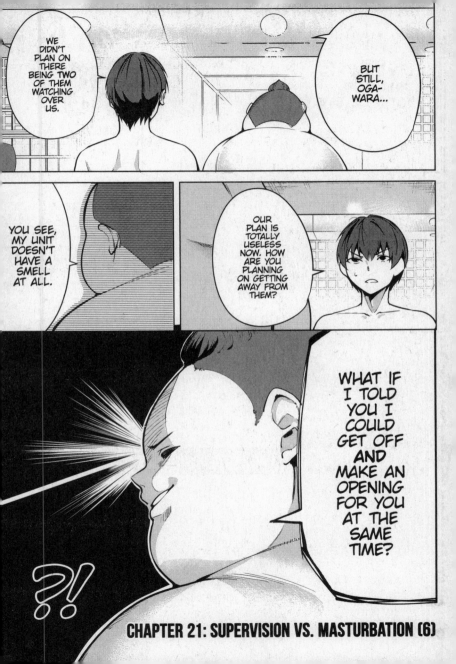

WE DIDN'T PLAN ON THERE BEING TWO OF THEM WATCHING OVER US.

BUT STILL, OGA-WARA...

YOU SEE, MY UNIT DOESN'T HAVE A SMELL AT ALL.

OUR PLAN IS TOTALLY USELESS NOW. HOW ARE YOU PLANNING ON GETTING AWAY FROM THEM?

WHAT IF I TOLD YOU I COULD GET OFF AND MAKE AN OPENING FOR YOU AT THE SAME TIME?

CHAPTER 21: SUPERVISION VS. MASTURBATION (6)

H-HOLD ON. WHAT ARE YOU TALKING ABOUT?
WHEN THE TIME COMES, YOU'LL KNOW.
HEY, WAIT...!
THE HECK IS HE PLANNING TO DO?
WHOA!
SLIP...
ARE YOU OK, SUKE-KAWA?!
YEAH, I WASN'T PAYING ATTENTION. THE FAULT'S ALL MINE.

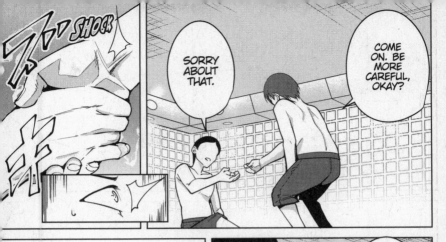

SHOCK

SORRY ABOUT THAT.

COME ON. BE MORE CAREFUL, OKAY?

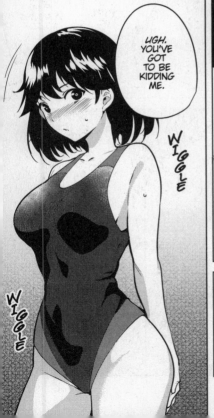

UGH. YOU'VE GOT TO BE KIDDING ME.

WIGGLE

WIGGLE

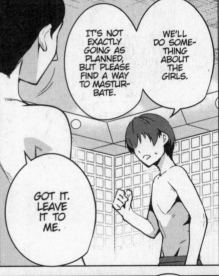

IT'S NOT EXACTLY GOING AS PLANNED, BUT PLEASE FIND A WAY TO MASTUR-BATE.

WE'LL DO SOME-THING ABOUT THE GIRLS.

GOT IT. LEAVE IT TO ME.

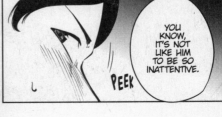

PEEK

YOU KNOW, IT'S NOT LIKE HIM TO BE SO INATTENTIVE.

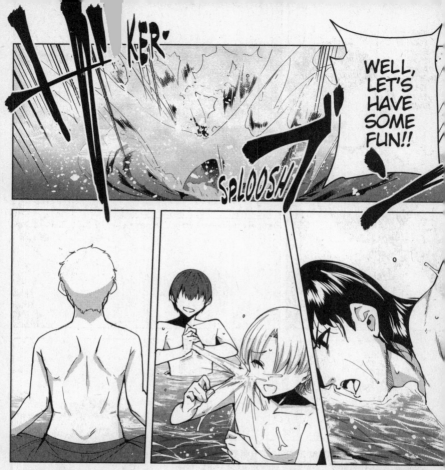

WELL, LET'S HAVE SOME FUN!!

SpLOOSH

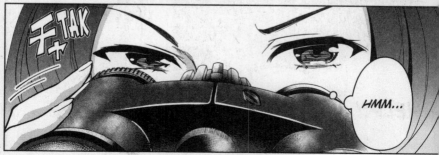

HMM...

148

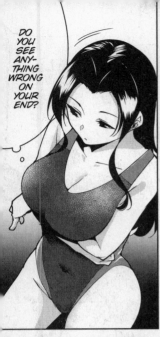

DO YOU SEE ANYTHING WRONG ON YOUR END?

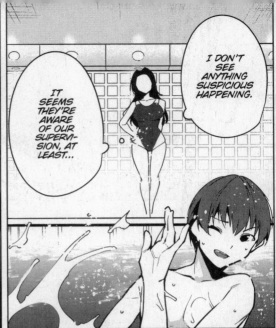

IT SEEMS THEY'RE AWARE OF OUR SUPERVISION, AT LEAST...

I DON'T SEE ANYTHING SUSPICIOUS HAPPENING.

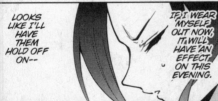

LOOKS LIKE I'LL HAVE THEM HOLD OFF ON--

IF I WEAR MYSELF OUT NOW, IT WILL HAVE AN EFFECT ON THIS EVENING.

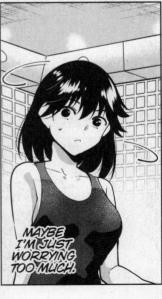

MAYBE I'M JUST WORRYING TOO MUCH.

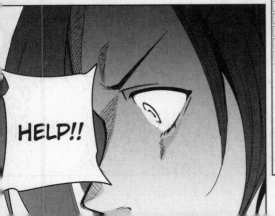

HELP!!

OGAWARA IS DROWN-ING!!
DD
SPLASH
GLUB
?!
MY LEG!
MY LEG'S CRAMP-ING!!
SPLOOSH
AN ACCIDENT?
SHUDDER...
OR A DIVERSION?
HEY! GIVE ME A HAND!
GOT IT!
YEAH, GRAB THAT FOR ME!
OKAY! NOW LIFT HIM UP HERE!
HOW COULD SOME-ONE BE SO DAMN HEAVY?!
MIT-SUKO-SAN, PLEASE, HELP!!
O-OKAY!

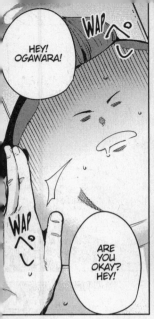

HEY! OGAWARA!

WAP ペ

WAP ペ

ARE YOU OKAY? HEY!

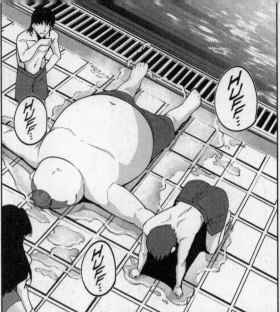

Hッ..

Hッ..

Hッ..

Hッ..

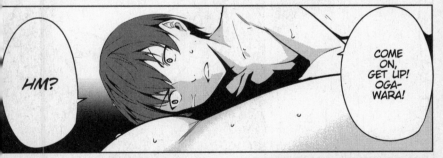

HM?

COME ON, GET UP! OGA-WARA!

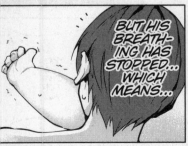

BUT HIS BREATH-ING HAS STOPPED... WHICH MEANS...

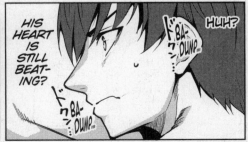

HIS HEART IS STILL BEAT-ING?

BA-DUMP...

BA-DUMP...

HUH?

FLICK
THAT'S RIGHT!
I CAN SEE IT NOW! WHAT YOU'RE AFTER!
MOUTH-TO-MOUTH!
HUH?
HE NEEDS MOUTH-TO-MOUTH!!
SOMEONE, HELP! HE ISN'T BREATH-ING!!

I DON'T KNOW HOW TO DO THAT.
NEITHER DO I. NEVER LEARNED.
I'LL DO IT.
!!
SERIOUSLY, MITSUKO?!
LUCKILY, I KNOW HOW TO DO CPR.
THERE'S A CHANCE THIS IS ALL JUST AN ACT...BUT IF IT ISN'T...
THERE'S NO WAY WE CAN LOSE ONE OF OUR FEW PRECIOUS VIRGINS!
DO FORGIVE ME.

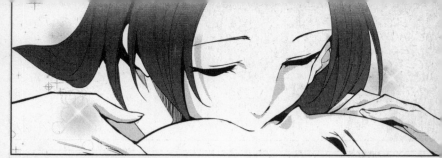

NOW, HOW ARE WE GOING TO USE THIS OPENING TO MAS- TURBATE?

OKAY, THIS SHOULD KEEP MITSUKO'S HANDS FULL FOR A BIT!

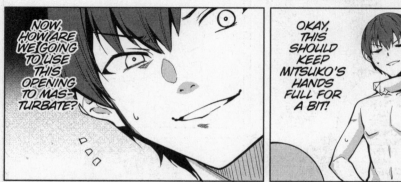

WIGGLE もぞ

WIGGLE もぞ

WILL WE MAKE IT?

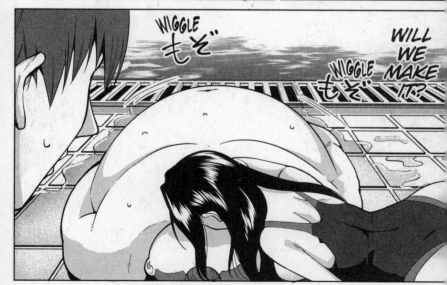

154

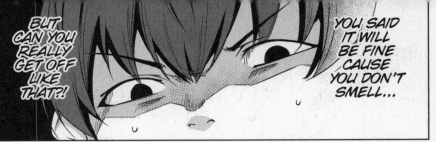

BUT CAN YOU REALLY GET OFF LIKE THAT!

YOU SAID IT WILL BE FINE CAUSE YOU DON'T SMELL...

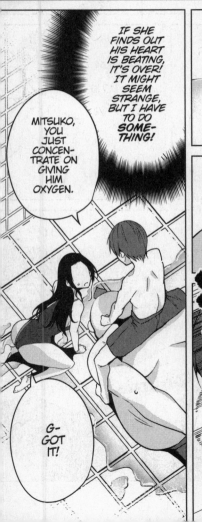

IF SHE FINDS OUT HIS HEART IS BEATING, IT'S OVER! IT MIGHT SEEM STRANGE, BUT I HAVE TO DO SOMETHING!

MITSUKO, YOU JUST CONCENTRATE ON GIVING HIM OXYGEN.

G-GOT IT!

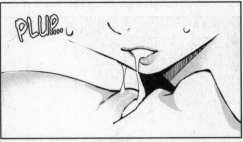

PLUP....

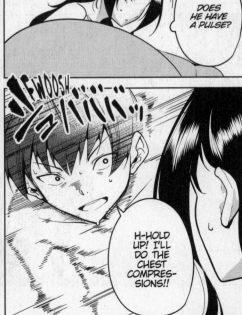

DOES HE HAVE A PULSE?

FEWOOSH....

H-HOLD UP! I'LL DO THE CHEST COMPRESSIONS!!

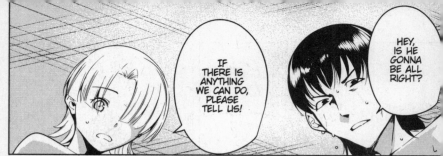

IF THERE IS ANYTHING WE CAN DO, PLEASE TELL US!

HEY, IS HE GONNA BE ALL RIGHT?

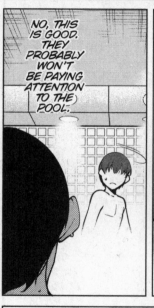

NO, THIS IS GOOD. THEY PROBABLY WON'T BE PAYING ATTENTION TO THE POOL.

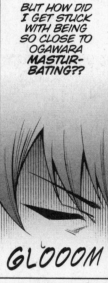

BUT HOW DID I GET STUCK WITH BEING SO CLOSE TO OGAWARA **MASTUR-BATING??**

GLOOOM

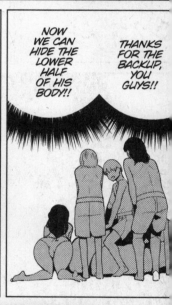

NOW WE CAN HIDE THE LOWER HALF OF HIS BODY!!

THANKS FOR THE BACKUP, YOU GUYS!!

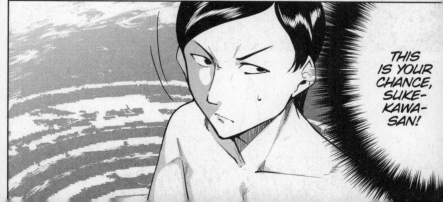

THIS IS YOUR CHANCE, SUKE-KAWA-SAN!

BLOOSH...
OW ...!
SHOCK
MY HAND WON'T MOVE THE WAY I WANT!!
DID I INJURE IT WHEN I FELL BEFORE?!
DAMN!! AT THIS RATE, I'M GOING TO MISS MY CHANCE!
DON'T MOVE, PLEASE.
SLIP

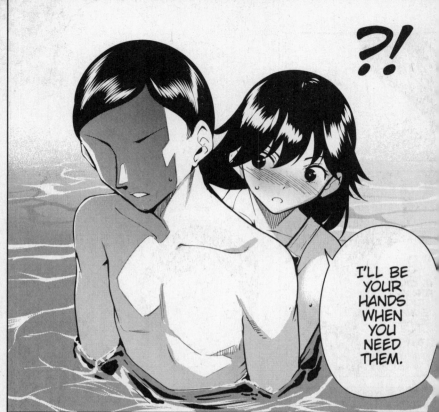

?!

I'LL BE YOUR HANDS WHEN YOU NEED THEM.

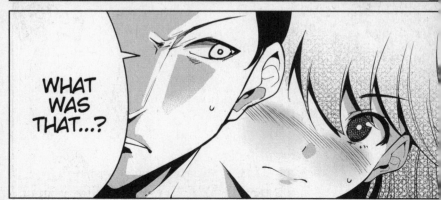

WHAT WAS THAT...?

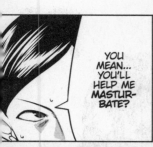

YOU MEAN... YOU'LL HELP ME MASTUR-BATE?

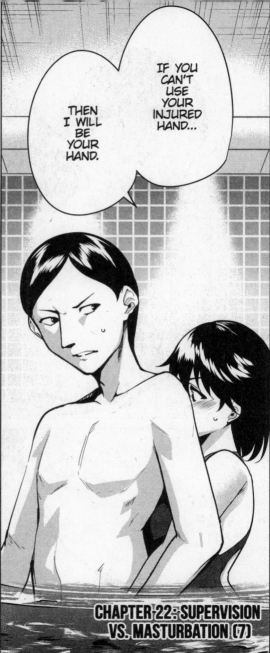

IF YOU CAN'T USE YOUR INJURED HAND...

THEN I WILL BE YOUR HAND.

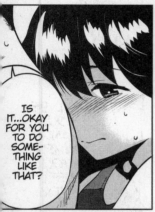

IS IT...OKAY FOR YOU TO DO SOME-THING LIKE THAT?

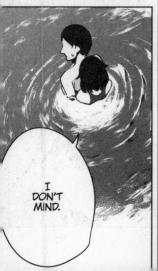

I DON'T MIND.

CHAPTER 22: SUPERVISION VS. MASTURBATION (7)

I...
I DON'T WANT YOU TO DIE.

BECAUSE...

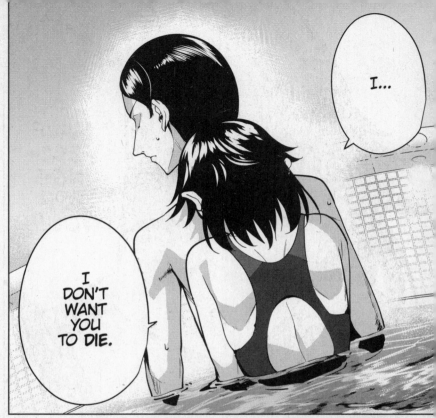

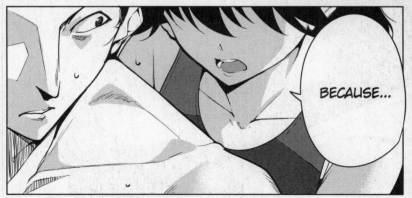

I HAVE FEEL-INGS FOR YOU!!
!!

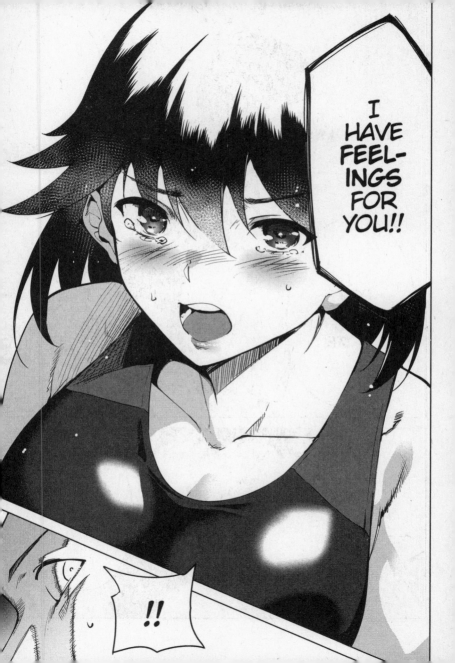

SHLUP...
シュル…ッ SHLUP...
~~…
JOLT
AH...!
SHLUP...
SQSH
SHLUP...
SHLIP...
AHH...
MM...! ♥
JOLT...

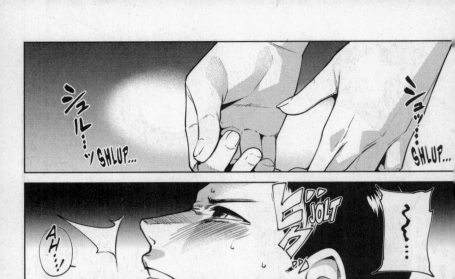

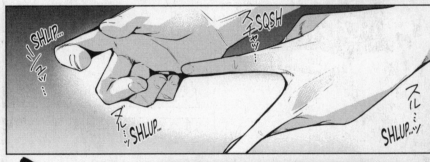

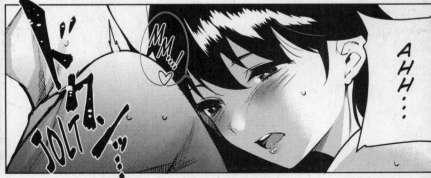

WELL, MITSUKO?
JERK
JERK
JERK
HE MOVED! I THINK HE'S BACK!
GUH-WHOO-OOAA!!
JOLT

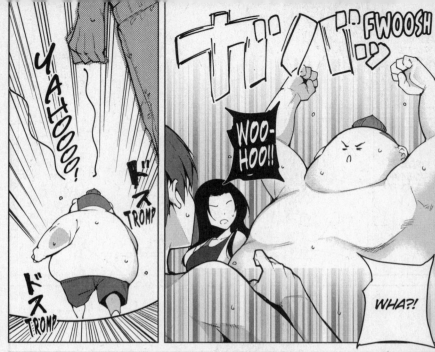

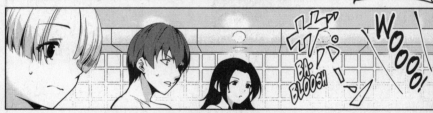

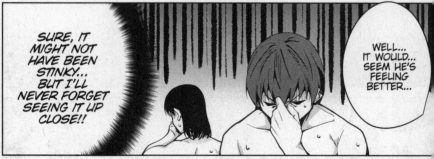

SURE, IT MIGHT NOT HAVE BEEN STINKY... BUT I'LL NEVER FORGET SEEING IT UP CLOSE!!

WELL... IT WOULD... SEEM HE'S FEELING BETTER...

OGAWARA, HOW ARE YOU FEELING?
GOOD! I MADE SURE TO CLEAN AWAY ALL THE EVIDENCE IN THE POOL!
THE POOL... THAT'S RIGHT!!
GASP!
SUKE-KAWA-SAN?!
SUKE-KAWA-SAN!!
......
!!
GULP...

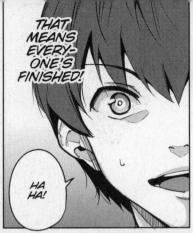

THAT MEANS EVERY-ONE'S FINISHED!

HA HA!

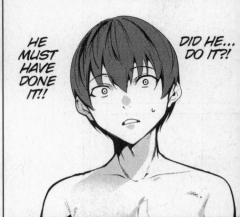

HE MUST HAVE DONE IT!!

DID HE... DO IT?!

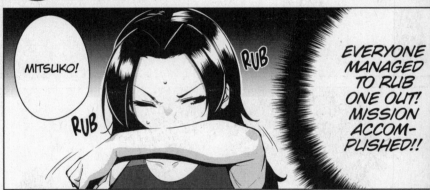

MITSUKO!

RUB

RUB

EVERYONE MANAGED TO RUB ONE OUT! MISSION ACCOM-PLISHED!!

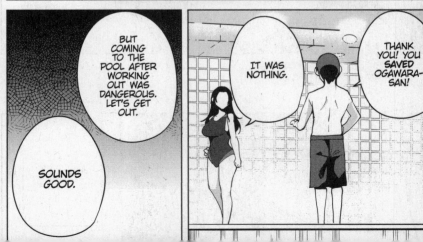

BUT COMING TO THE POOL AFTER WORKING OUT WAS DANGEROUS. LET'S GET OUT.

SOUNDS GOOD.

IT WAS NOTHING.

THANK YOU! YOU SAVED OGAWARA-SAN!

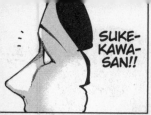

SUKE-KAWA-SAN!!

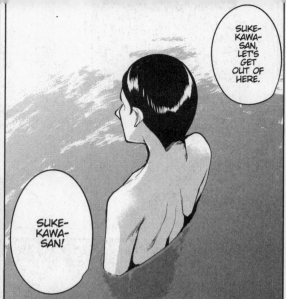

SUKE-KAWA-SAN, LET'S GET OUT OF HERE.

SUKE-KAWA-SAN!

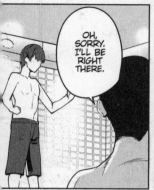

OH, SORRY. I'LL BE RIGHT THERE.

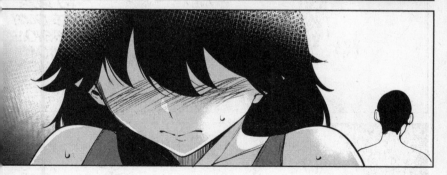

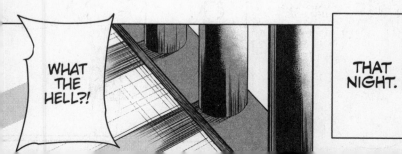

WHAT THE HELL?!

THAT NIGHT.

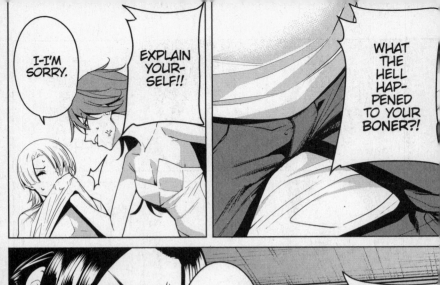

WHAT THE HELL HAPPENED TO YOUR BONER?!
EXPLAIN YOURSELF!!
I-I'M SORRY.
MITSUKO, THIS ONE'S NO GOOD, EITHER!
......!
SORRY, MITSUKO...
IT LOOKS LIKE MY IMPOTENCE CAME BACK, OR SOMETHING.
BUT HOW...?!

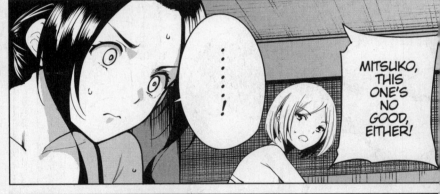

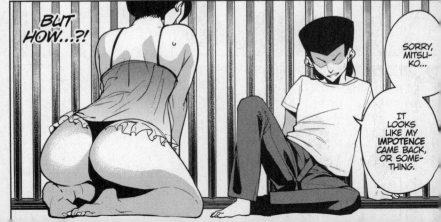

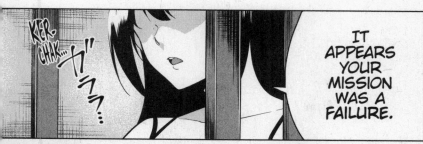

KER CHAK... ブ二ブ...

IT APPEARS YOUR MISSION WAS A FAILURE.

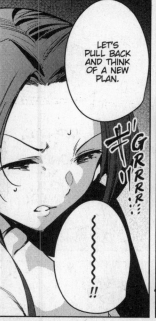

LET'S PULL BACK AND THINK OF A NEW PLAN.

#'GRRRR...

!!

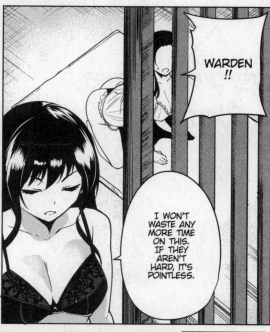

WARDEN!!

I WON'T WASTE ANY MORE TIME ON THIS. IF THEY AREN'T HARD, IT'S POINTLESS.

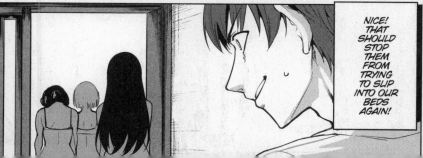

NICE! THAT SHOULD STOP THEM FROM TRYING TO SLIP INTO OUR BEDS AGAIN!

THANK YOU, SAYAKA-CHAN.
IT'S ALL THANKS TO YOU!
SAYAKA-CH--
WHAP
?!
EH?! HUH?! WHY DID SHE LOOK AT ME LIKE THAT?!
Y-YOU'RE THE ONE WHO TOLD ME TO MASTUR-BATE!

MUR MUR...
DISGUST-ING...
UH...
WHAAAT?
I HAVE NO IDEA WHAT THEY COULD'VE DONE...
BUT TO THINK THEY COULD GET BY MITSUKO.
AINA... HOW MUCH LONGER?
CLANK...
CLANK...

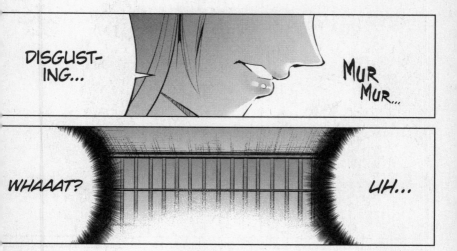

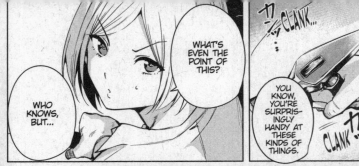

WHAT'S EVEN THE POINT OF THIS?

WHO KNOWS, BUT...

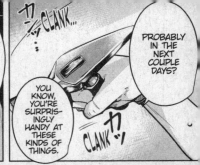

カッ CLANK...

YOU KNOW, YOU'RE SURPRISINGLY HANDY AT THESE KINDS OF THINGS.

PROBABLY IN THE NEXT COUPLE DAYS?

CLANK カッ

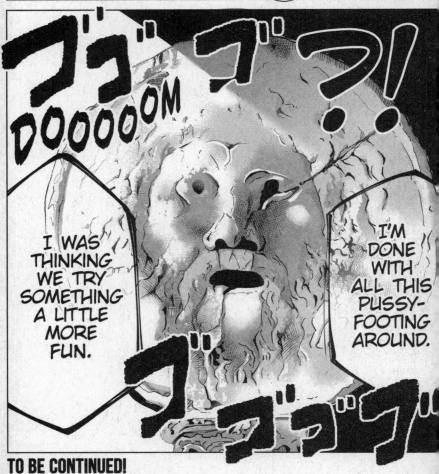

I WAS THINKING WE TRY SOMETHING A LITTLE MORE FUN.

I'M DONE WITH ALL THIS PUSSY-FOOTING AROUND.

TO BE CONTINUED!

DESTINY LOVERS

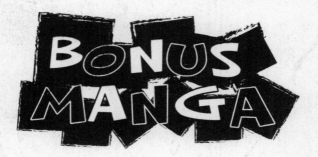

BONUS MANGA

DESTINY LOVERS
02

IMMEDIATELY AFTER THE PLAN TO SLEEP WITH THE BOYS FAILED...
SHA HAA
TAAAA
PLIP...
CREAK

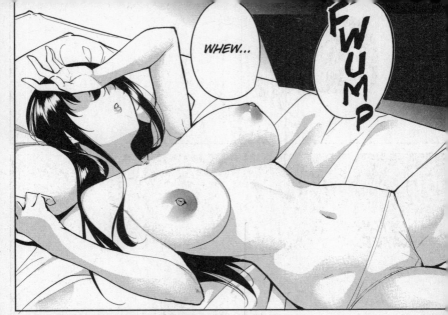

WHEW...

FWUMP

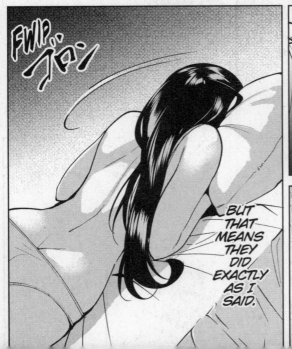

FWIP

BUT THAT MEANS THEY DID EXACTLY AS I SAID.

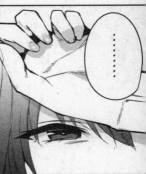

. . . .

I'M HAPPY THAT KOSUKE-KUN AND THE OTHERS WERE ABLE TO FIND A WAY...

THEY ALL... MASTUR-BATED.
EVEN KOSUKE-KUN...
MASTUR-BATED.
......
I WONDER...
SLLLFFF
HAAH...
WHAT DID HE THINK ABOUT ...?
HAAH...

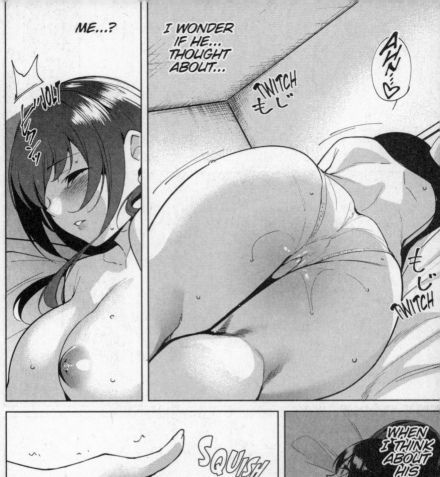

ME...?

I WONDER IF HE... THOUGHT ABOUT...

TWITCH
もじ

AN...♡

もじ
TWITCH

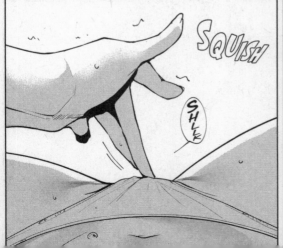

SQUISH

SHLK

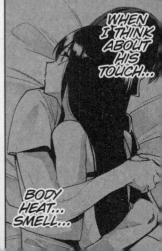

WHEN I THINK ABOUT HIS TOUCH...

BODY HEAT... SMELL...

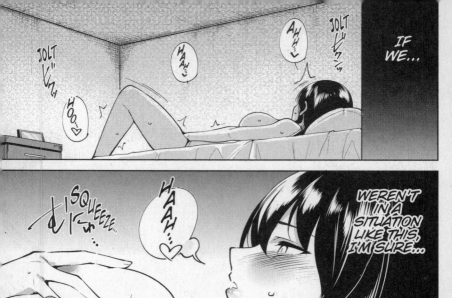

IF WE...

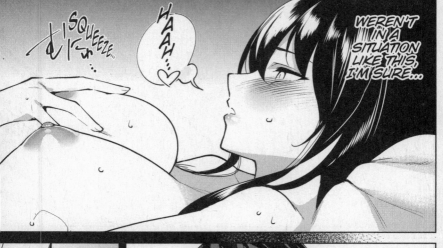

WEREN'T IN A SITUATION LIKE THIS, I'M SURE...

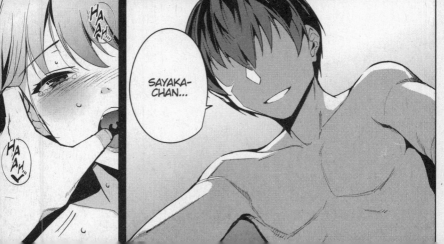

SAYAKA-CHAN...

YOU DON'T NEED TO BE SO SHY.
STO-- ♡
TWEAK TWEAK
SHLURP
YAAAH...!! ♡
JOLT
HAAH! AHHH! ♡ ♡
JOLT

AHNN!!♡
SHLK
...♡
SHLK
STOP... DON'T LOOK...♡
BUT, YOU'RE SO BEAUTIFUL, SAYAKA-CHAN.
SQUISH
SQUOOSH
SHLRRRP...
AH!♡
JOLT...
KO-SUKE... KUN...♡
JOLT...

JOLT
JOLT
JOLT
HAAAAH...♥
HAAAH...
HAAH!♥
HAAH...
HAAH...
HAAH...
KOSUKE...
KUN...
FIN

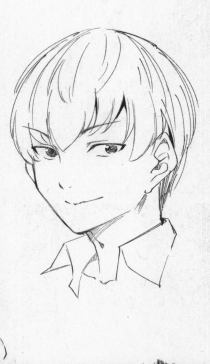

Fujishiro Kosuke

藤代康介

DESTINY LOVERS CHARACTER FILE 06

Childhood friends with Sayaka.
However, he was called a woman-hater
by his classmates. In reality,
he's a virgin because of the promise
he made as a kid with Sayaka.

6'4"
6'2"
6'0"
5'10"
5'8"
5'6"
5'4"
5'2"
5'0"
4'1"
4'8"
4'6"
4'4"
4'2"
4'0"
3'10"
3'8"
3'6"

Irabu Kazuchika

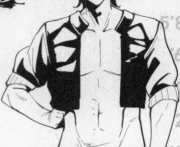

伊良部和親

DESTINY LOVERS CHARACTER FILE 07

Projects the attitude of a tough-guy delinquent. Kind of dumb, but good at fighting. Not exactly unattractive to more rough-and-tumble girls, but he always rejected them. His excuse? "I ain't got time to waste on chicks." In reality, he's impotent, which is the reason for his virginity.

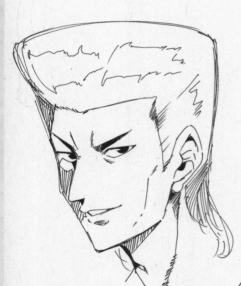

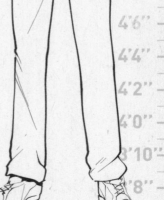

6'4"

6'2"

6'0"

5'10"

5'8"

5'6"

5'4"

5'2"

5'0"

4'10"

4'8"

4'6"

4'4"

4'2"

4'0"

3'10"

3'8"

3'6"

3'4"

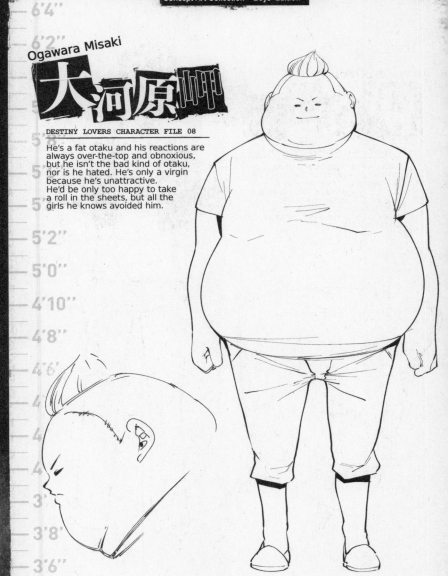

Ogawara Misaki

大河原岬

DESTINY LOVERS CHARACTER FILE 08

He's a fat otaku and his reactions are always over-the-top and obnoxious, but he isn't the bad kind of otaku, nor is he hated. He's only a virgin because he's unattractive. He'd be only too happy to take a roll in the sheets, but all the girls he knows avoided him.

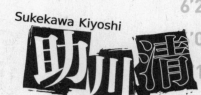

Sukekawa Kiyoshi

助川清

DESTINY LOVERS CHARACTER FILE 09

A glasses-wearing, high-class, white-collar worker. Cool, indifferent, and analytical, he's no good with women and a germaphobe to boot, so he's still a virgin. He inadvertently causes some girls to cry by calling them dirty and smelly.

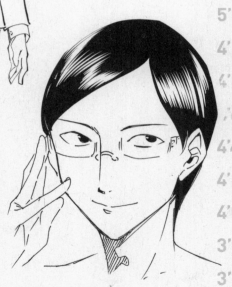

6'4"
6'2"
6'0"
5'10"
5'8"
5'6"
5'4"
5'2"
5'0"
4'10"
4'8"
4'6"
4'4"
4'2"
4'0"
3'10"
3'8"
3'6"
3'4"

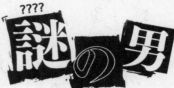

????

謎の男

DESTINY LOVERS CHARACTER FILE 10

He doesn't say too much, not even his name. No one has any idea what he's thinking. The reason for his virginity is unknown.

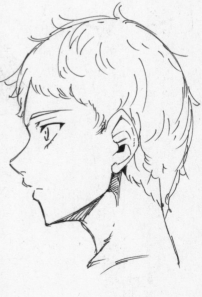

Kazamatsuri Shunta

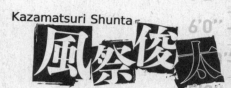

DESTINY LOVERS CHARACTER FILE 11

A young man who comes off rather effeminate. He is kind and gentle. You'd think he would be rather appealing to the right kind of person...but at this stage, we don't know why he's a virgin.

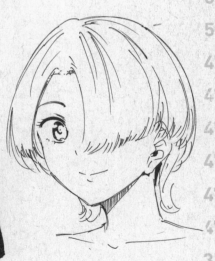

6'4"
6'2"
6'0"
5'8"
5'6"
5'4"
5'2"
5'0"
4'10"
4'8"
4'6"
4'4"
4'2"
4'0"
3'10"
3'8"
3'6"

DESTINY LOVERS

NEXT TIME
This time......
Attack in the Haunted House ?!
HAUNTED HOUSE
YOU ALL WILL VENTURE INTO THE HAUNTED HOUSE.
WE MADE THIS ESPE-CIALLY FOR YOU.
Traps on traps !!
Lust on lust !!
DAMN IT...! I CAN'T GET IT OUT!!
I KNEW THIS WAS ONE OF YOUR TRAPS!
They can't hold back ...!!
DA- DUN
DA- DUN
SEE... ONCE YOU DECIDE TO STOP LYING TO YOURSELF, PERHAPS YOU CAN GO FREE?
DRIP...

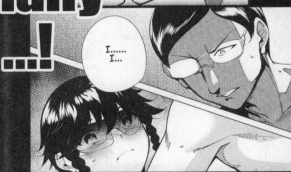

And
Sukekawa...

finally
...!

Destiny Lovers Volume 3 is coming soon!

SEVEN SEAS' GHOST SHIP PRESENTS

DESTINY LOVERS

story by **KAZUTAKA**   art by **KAI TOMOHIRO**   VOLUME 2

TRANSLATION
Thomas Zimmerman

ADAPTATION
Steven Golebiewski

LETTERING AND RETOUCH
Ludwig Sacramento

COVER DESIGN
Nicky Lim

PROOFREADER
Elise Kelsey

EDITOR
J.P. Sullivan

PREPRESS TECHNICIAN
Rhiannon Rasmussen-Silverstein

PRODUCTION MANAGER
Lissa Pattillo

MANAGING EDITOR
Julie Davis

ASSOCIATE PUBLISHER
Adam Arnold

PUBLISHER
Jason DeAngelis

DESTINY LOVERS VOLUME 2
© Kazutaka / Kai Tomohiro 2018
All rights reserved.
First published in Japan in 2018 by Kodansha Ltd., Tokyo.
Publication rights for this English edition arranged through Kodansha Ltd., Tokyo.

Seven Seas press and purchase enquiries can be sent to Marketing Manager Lianne Sentar at press@gomanga.com. Information regarding the distribution and purchase of digital editions is available from Digital Manager CK Russell at digital@gomanga.com.

Seven Seas, Ghost Ship, and their accompanying logos are trademarks of Seven Seas Entertainment. All rights reserved.

ISBN: 978-1-947804-68-5

Printed in Canada

First Printing: February 2020

10 9 8 7 6 5 4 3 2 1

FOLLOW US ONLINE: www.ghostshipmanga.com

READING DIRECTIONS

This book reads from *right to left*, Japanese style. If this is your first time reading manga, you start reading from the top right panel on each page and take it from there. If you get lost, just follow the numbered diagram here. It may seem backwards at first, but you'll get the hang of it! Have fun!!

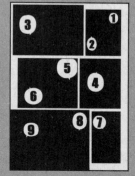